JACKSON SAND

GLADIATOR 2
MOVIE
EVERYTHING YOU NEED TO KNOW

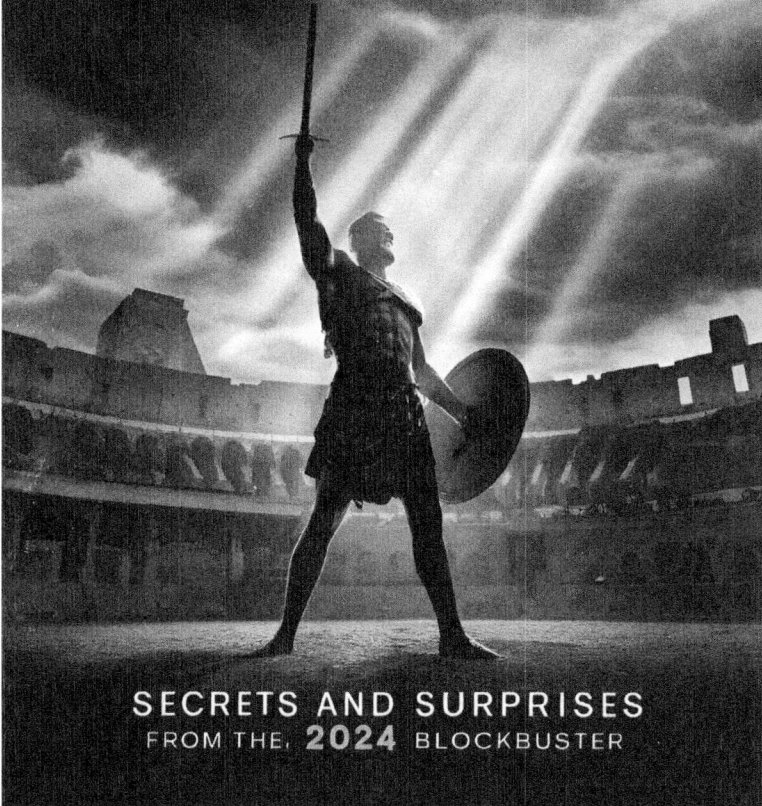

SECRETS AND SURPRISES
FROM THE 2024 BLOCKBUSTER

Gladiator 2 Movie: Everything You Need to Know

Secrets and Surprises from the 2024 Blockbuster

By

Jackson Sanderson

TABLE OF CONTENT

Introduction

Welcome Note

Welcome, dear reader, to an odyssey of anticipation, intrigue, and cinematic splendor. We stand on the precipice of a monumental moment in film history, eagerly awaiting the release of "Gladiator 2," the 2024 blockbuster that promises to reignite the flames of an epic saga. As you hold this book in your hands, you embark on a journey through the labyrinth of creativity, dedication, and passion that brings this monumental sequel to life. This is more than a guide; it is a treasure trove of secrets, surprises, and everything you need to know about the cinematic marvel that is "Gladiator 2."

Two decades have passed since Ridley Scott's "Gladiator" graced our screens, captivating audiences worldwide with its visceral portrayal of honor, vengeance, and the unyielding human spirit. The tale of Maximus Decimus Meridius, the general-turned-gladiator, became an instant classic, leaving an indelible mark on popular culture. Now, as the drums of war beat once more, we find ourselves on the cusp of returning to the sands of the Colosseum, eager to witness the next chapter of this legendary story.

But what is it about "Gladiator 2" that stirs such excitement and anticipation? Why has the announcement of this sequel sent ripples of exhilaration through the hearts of moviegoers and critics alike? To answer these questions, we must delve deep into the very essence of what makes this film a cultural phenomenon. This book is your gateway to understanding the magic behind the making of "Gladiator 2," unraveling the secrets and surprises that await you in the theaters.

As we navigate through the chapters ahead, you'll uncover the intricate tapestry of the film's production. From the early whispers of its development to the final, thunderous applause at its premiere, every step of this cinematic journey is meticulously chronicled. You'll meet the visionary minds behind the scenes—directors, producers, screenwriters—whose collective genius breathes life into the epic. Their stories are woven with threads of creativity, ambition, and an unrelenting drive to create something truly extraordinary.

And then, there are the stars—the luminous constellation of talent that assembles to bring this story to life. Familiar faces return, their characters etched into our memories, while new heroes and villains emerge, each with a tale to tell. We'll explore the motivations, challenges, and triumphs of these actors, offering you a glimpse into the heart of their performances. Through their eyes, you'll see the world of "Gladiator 2" not just as a spectator, but as an insider, privy to the emotions and experiences that shape this epic narrative.

The plot of "Gladiator 2" remains shrouded in mystery, a tantalizing enigma that fuels countless speculations and fan theories. In this book, we gather the pieces of this puzzle, presenting you with confirmed details, educated guesses, and wild imaginations. The thrill of discovery is yours to savor as we peel back the layers of this story, revealing the core of what promises to be an unforgettable cinematic experience.

Our journey wouldn't be complete without a tour of the film's breathtaking locations and stunning production design. The visual grandeur of "Gladiator 2" is a feast for the senses, meticulously crafted to transport you to a world where the past and the present collide in spectacular fashion. From the majestic Colosseum to the expansive landscapes, every frame is a work of art, a testament to the skill and dedication of the filmmakers.

Special effects and cinematography have evolved leaps and bounds since the original "Gladiator" graced our screens. The technological advancements employed in "Gladiator 2" promise to elevate the spectacle to unprecedented heights. We delve into the marvels of modern filmmaking, exploring how cutting-edge techniques blend with timeless storytelling to create a visual masterpiece.

Music, too, plays a pivotal role in this epic. The haunting melodies and powerful scores that underscored the original film's most poignant moments are etched into our collective consciousness. In this sequel, the music promises to soar even higher, capturing the essence of the story and amplifying its emotional resonance. We'll examine the work of the composers, the inspiration behind the music, and the unforgettable themes that will linger in your mind long after the credits roll.

Marketing and promotion are the lifeblood of any blockbuster, and "Gladiator 2" is no exception. The trailers, teasers, and campaigns build a crescendo of excitement, drawing audiences into the fold. We analyze these strategies, dissecting the elements that make them effective and exploring how they shape our perceptions and expectations.

As the release date approaches, the world buzzes with anticipation. The dichotomy of theatrical versus streaming releases adds a layer of intrigue, reflecting the changing landscape of film consumption. We'll provide you with the latest information, ensuring you're up to date with all the critical details. Premiere events and early reviews will set the stage for the film's reception, and we capture the essence of these moments in vivid detail.

The voices of the fans are a symphony of excitement, critique, and creative expression. Social media buzz, early reviews, and fan art create a tapestry of community engagement that enriches the film's narrative. We'll showcase this vibrant ecosystem, highlighting the myriad ways in which fans interact with and contribute to the world of "Gladiator 2."

Finally, we reflect on the impact of "Gladiator" on pop culture and speculate on the legacy of its sequel. The original film's influence is undeniable, and "Gladiator 2" is poised to leave its own indelible mark. What does the future hold for this franchise? Our concluding chapter offers thoughtful predictions and reflections, leaving you with much to ponder as you await the film's release.

So, dear reader, prepare yourself for a journey of epic proportions. "Gladiator 2 Movie: Everything You Need to Know – Secrets and Surprises from the 2024 Blockbuster" is your companion, guide, and confidant. Together, we will traverse the realms of ancient Rome, uncover the mysteries of the Colosseum, and stand shoulder to shoulder with heroes and villains alike. The stage is set, the actors are ready, and the world is waiting. Let us begin.

Why This Book

Why, you might ask, do we need another book about a movie, even if that movie is as eagerly anticipated as "Gladiator 2"? In a world where information is just a click away, where trailers, interviews, and endless speculation fill our screens, what can this humble book offer that your smartphone cannot? The answer, dear reader, lies in the magic of storytelling and the power of a well-crafted narrative to bring depth, understanding, and a sense of shared excitement to something we all look forward to: the return of a cinematic legend.

"Gladiator 2 Movie: Everything You Need to Know – Secrets and Surprises from the 2024 Blockbuster" is not just a compilation of facts and figures. It is a journey, a companion that walks alongside you as we explore the making of this epic film. Think of it as a trusted friend who shares not only the details but the heart and soul of the story behind the story. It's like sitting by a warm fire, listening to tales spun with care, passion, and an eye for the extraordinary.

Movies are more than just entertainment; they are cultural touchstones that resonate with us on a deep level. The original "Gladiator" was one such film, a sweeping epic that captured the imagination of millions. Its legacy has endured, and the anticipation for its sequel is a testament to its impact. But how do we navigate the sea of information, the tide of rumors, and the wave of official updates? This book serves as your anchor, providing a structured, comprehensive, and engaging exploration of everything that makes "Gladiator 2" a phenomenon worth celebrating.

Firstly, let's talk about the significance of the information provided. This book is not a mere rehash of press releases or a collection of speculative articles. It is meticulously researched, drawing from a wide array of sources to bring you the most accurate, up-to-date, and insightful content possible. You will find exclusive behind-the-scenes glimpses, in-depth analyses, and thoughtful commentary that go beyond the surface. It's about peeling back the layers to reveal the intricate craftsmanship that goes into making a blockbuster film. From the visionaries who conceive the story to the artisans who build the sets, every facet of the production process is illuminated.

In the chapters that follow, we dive deep into the world of "Gladiator 2." You'll learn about the development history of the film, tracing its journey from concept to screen. This is not just a list of dates and events but a narrative that captures the challenges, triumphs, and creative processes that shaped the movie. You'll meet the key players—directors, producers, and screenwriters—whose combined talents have breathed life into this project. Their stories, filled with passion and dedication, add a human touch to the monumental task of creating a sequel to a beloved classic.

The cast and characters are, of course, a central focus. "Gladiator 2" brings together a stellar ensemble of actors, some returning, some new, each bringing their unique flair to the story. This book provides detailed profiles of these characters, exploring their motivations, arcs, and how they fit into the broader narrative. You'll gain insights into the performances that promise to bring these characters to life in ways that are both familiar and refreshingly new. It's about understanding the heartbeats behind the faces we see on screen.

Plot and storyline are the core of any great film, and "Gladiator 2" is no exception. While much of the plot remains under wraps, this book offers a careful balance of confirmed details, thoughtful speculation, and fan theories. It's a tantalizing mix that keeps you on the edge of your seat, eagerly anticipating what's to come. By understanding the story's roots in the original film and its new directions, you'll appreciate the narrative's depth and complexity even more.

Filming locations and production design are more than just backdrops—they are characters in their own right. The aesthetic choices, the painstaking attention to detail, and the immersive environments all contribute to the film's authenticity and emotional impact. This book takes you on a visual tour of these locations, offering behind-the-scenes insights that enrich your viewing experience. You'll see how modern technology and timeless craftsmanship combine to create a world that feels both ancient and immediate.

Special effects and cinematography have evolved dramatically since the original "Gladiator." This sequel leverages cutting-edge techniques to create breathtaking visuals and compelling action sequences. Understanding these advancements enhances your appreciation of the film's technical prowess. This book breaks down these elements in an accessible way, making the complex world of VFX and cinematography understandable and fascinating.

Music is the soul of "Gladiator 2," as it was for its predecessor. The score's ability to evoke emotion, set the tone, and enhance the narrative is unparalleled. This book delves into the composition process, exploring how themes are developed and woven into the fabric of the story. You'll gain a deeper appreciation for the musical genius behind the film, understanding how every note contributes to the overall experience.

Marketing and promotion are the engines that drive a film's success. Trailers, teasers, and campaigns build the excitement and anticipation that culminate in the film's release. This book examines these strategies, offering a critical look at how they shape audience expectations and enhance the film's reach. It's about understanding the machinery behind the magic.

As the release date approaches, the buzz grows louder. Social media buzz, early reviews, and fan art all contribute to the cultural conversation. This book captures this excitement, providing a snapshot of the collective anticipation and creative expressions that surround "Gladiator 2." It's a celebration of the community that makes filmgoing a shared, vibrant experience.

In the end, this book is about more than just a movie. It's about the passion, creativity, and human spirit that drive us to tell stories, to create worlds, and to connect with one another through the shared experience of cinema. "Gladiator 2 Movie: Everything You Need to Know – Secrets and Surprises from the 2024 Blockbuster" is your guide to this epic journey. It's a labor of love, crafted with care to ensure that you, the reader, are not just informed but deeply engaged, eagerly anticipating the moment when the lights dim, the screen glows, and the magic of "Gladiator 2" unfolds before your eyes.

So, whether you're a die-hard fan of the original or a newcomer eager to experience the spectacle, this book is for you. It's a celebration, an exploration, and above all, an invitation to be a part of something truly extraordinary. Welcome to the world of "Gladiator 2." Let the journey begin.

The Legacy of Gladiator

Once upon a time in the vast and bustling world of cinema, a film emerged that was destined to carve its name into the annals of history. That film was "Gladiator," a masterpiece directed by Ridley Scott, released in the year 2000. From the moment the first note of Hans Zimmer's iconic score echoed through theaters, audiences knew they were witnessing something extraordinary. "Gladiator" was not just a movie; it was an epic tale of honor, vengeance, and redemption, set against the brutal and breathtaking backdrop of ancient Rome. It was a story that resonated deeply with audiences and critics alike, leaving an indelible mark on the world of film.

The journey begins with Maximus Decimus Meridius, a character portrayed with unparalleled intensity and grace by Russell Crowe. Maximus, a general betrayed and forced into slavery, rises to become a gladiator who defies an emperor. His quest for vengeance against the treacherous Commodus, played with chilling brilliance by Joaquin Phoenix, is the beating heart of the narrative. The film's storyline is a tapestry of loyalty, betrayal, love, and loss, woven with threads of visceral combat and poignant emotion.

"Gladiator" was a critical triumph, garnering accolades and awards across the globe. It won five Academy Awards, including Best Picture and Best Actor for Crowe. The film's success was a testament to its powerful storytelling, impeccable direction, and stellar performances. Critics praised its epic scale, the depth of its characters, and the sheer emotional weight it carried. It was a film that struck a chord with the audience, resonating on both a personal and universal level.

Commercially, "Gladiator" was a juggernaut. It grossed over $460 million worldwide, a staggering sum at the time, solidifying its status as a blockbuster. But beyond the box office numbers, it was the cultural impact of "Gladiator" that truly set it apart. It reignited public interest in historical epics, a genre that had seen dwindling attention in the years prior. The film's success paved the way for a resurgence of interest in ancient Rome and historical storytelling in cinema.

The influence of "Gladiator" on pop culture is profound and enduring. Maximus's stirring speeches, his rallying cry of "Are you not entertained?" have become part of the cultural lexicon. The film's dialogue, scenes, and even its aesthetic have been referenced and parodied in countless other works, from television shows to advertising campaigns. It inspired a new generation of filmmakers and actors, demonstrating the power of a well-crafted epic to capture the imagination and hearts of audiences worldwide.

Ridley Scott's vision for "Gladiator" was grand and meticulous. He recreated the world of ancient Rome with painstaking detail, using a blend of practical effects and cutting-edge CGI to bring the Colosseum and other iconic locations to life. The film's production design, costuming, and visual effects were groundbreaking, setting new standards for historical accuracy and visual storytelling. It was a visual feast, a spectacle that transported viewers to a time long past yet made it feel immediate and real.

The film's music, composed by Hans Zimmer and Lisa Gerrard, is another key element of its lasting legacy. The haunting and evocative score, with its blend of orchestral and vocal elements, underscored the film's emotional highs and lows. The music of "Gladiator" is as iconic as its visuals, with themes that have become instantly recognizable. The soundtrack became a best-seller, further cementing the film's cultural footprint.

Beyond its technical and artistic achievements, "Gladiator" also sparked a renewed interest in the historical epic genre. Following its success, there was a noticeable increase in films and television series set in ancient Rome and other historical periods. "Gladiator" showed that there was a robust audience appetite for well-told stories from the past, inspiring a wave of historical dramas and epics in its wake.

The character of Maximus himself became a symbol of resilience and honor. His journey from general to slave to champion gladiator was a powerful narrative of overcoming adversity and fighting for justice. Maximus's story was one of personal loss and redemption, a timeless tale that resonated with audiences on a deep emotional level. His character arc was both tragic and triumphant, embodying the virtues of courage, loyalty, and integrity.

As we look forward to "Gladiator 2," it is this legacy that the sequel builds upon. The anticipation for the new film is rooted in the profound impact of the original. Fans of "Gladiator" are eager to return to the world that Ridley Scott and his team so masterfully created. They are excited to see how the story continues, to reconnect with beloved characters, and to be introduced to new ones. The legacy of "Gladiator" is a foundation of excellence and emotional depth, setting high expectations for the sequel.

"Gladiator" also had a significant influence on the careers of those involved. Russell Crowe's portrayal of Maximus catapulted him to international stardom, earning him widespread acclaim and numerous awards. Ridley Scott's direction was lauded, reaffirming his status as one of the great filmmakers of his generation. The film's success opened doors for many of its cast and crew, leaving a lasting impact on their professional lives.

The themes of "Gladiator" are timeless, resonating with audiences across different cultures and eras. The story's exploration of power, corruption, and redemption is universal, appealing to the shared human experience. Maximus's fight against tyranny and his quest for justice are narratives that continue to inspire and move audiences. "Gladiator" is more than just a film; it is a powerful storytelling experience that speaks to the core of what it means to be human.

As we stand on the brink of "Gladiator 2," we carry with us the legacy of its predecessor. The original film set a high bar, not only in terms of technical achievement and storytelling but also in its emotional and cultural impact. It is a legacy of excellence, one that the sequel aspires to honor and build upon. The world of "Gladiator" is rich with potential, its story far from over, and the anticipation for what comes next is a testament to the enduring power of this epic tale.

In conclusion, "Gladiator" is a film that has left an indelible mark on the film industry and popular culture. Its success, both critical and commercial, is a reflection of its exceptional storytelling, technical prowess, and emotional depth. The legacy of "Gladiator" is one of excellence, inspiring filmmakers, actors, and audiences alike. As we look forward to "Gladiator 2," we do so with a sense of excitement and reverence, eager to see how this epic story will continue to unfold. The journey of Maximus Decimus Meridius may have ended, but the world of "Gladiator" lives on, ready to captivate and inspire a new generation.

Anticipation for Gladiator 2

In the vast, star-studded cosmos of cinema, there are few announcements that can send ripples of excitement through the hearts of fans and critics alike. The confirmation of "Gladiator 2" is one such announcement, a beacon of light that has pierced the quotidian fabric of the movie industry, igniting imaginations and stirring anticipation to a fever pitch. It's a moment that feels both inevitable and miraculous, as if the very gods of storytelling have conspired to bring us back to the sands of the Colosseum for another grand spectacle.

The buzz began with a whisper, a tantalizing hint dropped in an interview or perhaps a cryptic tweet from someone in the know. It was the kind of news that felt too good to be true—after all, how could one hope to follow the monumental success of "Gladiator"? Yet, as whispers grew into murmurs and murmurs into shouts, it became clear that this was no mere rumor. "Gladiator 2" was happening, and the world was ready to be entertained once more.

The announcement of "Gladiator 2" has been met with a blend of fervent excitement and cautious optimism. Fans of the original film, whose lives were indelibly marked by the tale of Maximus Decimus Meridius, felt a surge of nostalgia and hope. This was a chance to revisit a world that had captivated them, to once again feel the thrill of the arena, the weight of a hero's journey, and the visceral impact of a story well told. For many, the return to ancient Rome feels like coming home, albeit to a home filled with swords, sand, and the ever-present specter of destiny.

Critics, too, have been abuzz, their pens and keyboards alight with speculation and analysis. There is a palpable sense of curiosity: How will Ridley Scott, the visionary director who brought the original to life, navigate the treacherous waters of sequel-making? What new stories will emerge from the dust and blood of the arena? And how will the film balance the expectations of loyal fans with the need to chart new territory?

These questions are the fuel that keeps the fires of anticipation burning brightly.

Part of the excitement stems from the sheer audacity of the endeavor. "Gladiator" was a film that redefined the epic genre, a monumental achievement that garnered critical acclaim and commercial success. It set a high bar, not just in terms of storytelling and visual grandeur, but in its ability to connect with audiences on a deeply emotional level. The sequel must not only honor this legacy but also expand upon it, delving into new narratives and exploring fresh thematic ground. It's a daunting task, but one that has been met with enthusiasm by the creative minds behind the project.

The speculation about "Gladiator 2" has been as varied and vibrant as the legions of Rome itself. Fans and critics have taken to social media, forums, and editorial pages to voice their hopes and theories. Will the sequel follow the story of Lucius, the young boy from the original film, now grown and facing his own battles? Will it explore the political machinations of Rome, diving deeper into the intrigue and power struggles that defined the era? Or will it introduce entirely new characters, offering a fresh perspective on a familiar world? The possibilities are endless, and each new piece of information only adds to the excitement.

One of the most tantalizing aspects of the sequel is the return of Ridley Scott. The director's vision was instrumental in crafting the epic scale and emotional depth of "Gladiator," and his involvement in the sequel has been met with widespread approval. Scott's mastery of visual storytelling, his ability to blend grandeur with intimacy, and his knack for creating immersive, believable worlds are qualities that promise to elevate "Gladiator 2" to new heights. His return is a signal to fans that this project is in the hands of someone who understands the weight of its legacy and is committed to delivering a film that lives up to the original's towering reputation.

The cast of "Gladiator 2" has also been a major point of interest and speculation. The original film boasted a stellar ensemble, with Russell Crowe's iconic portrayal of Maximus at its heart. While Crowe's return is unlikely given the character's fate, the casting of new and returning characters is a hot topic. There is particular excitement around the potential involvement of actors who can bring the same level of intensity and gravitas to their roles. Each casting announcement is dissected and discussed, adding fuel to the already blazing fire of anticipation.

The plot, of course, remains one of the greatest mysteries and sources of excitement. While details have been kept under tight wraps, the snippets that have emerged suggest a story that is both familiar and refreshingly new. There is talk of epic battles, political intrigue, and deeply personal journeys, all set against the backdrop of a Rome that is at once majestic and brutal. The promise of uncovering new layers to the world of "Gladiator" is enough to keep fans on the edge of their seats, counting down the days until the film's release.

Another reason for the high anticipation is the advances in technology since the original film was made. "Gladiator" was a groundbreaking achievement in its use of CGI and practical effects, but the tools available to filmmakers today are even more sophisticated. This means that "Gladiator 2" has the potential to offer even more stunning visuals, more immersive environments, and more dynamic action sequences. The thought of seeing the grandeur of ancient Rome brought to life with today's technology is a thrilling prospect, promising a visual feast that will captivate audiences.

Marketing and promotional strategies have also played a significant role in building excitement for the sequel. Trailers and teasers have been crafted with precision, each one designed to reveal just enough to tantalize without giving too much away. The careful drip-feed of information keeps the audience engaged, creating a sense of shared anticipation and community. Every poster, every snippet of footage, every interview with the cast and crew adds to the tapestry of excitement, weaving a narrative that draws fans in and keeps them hooked.

The social media buzz surrounding "Gladiator 2" is another testament to its high anticipation. Platforms like Twitter, Instagram, and Reddit are ablaze with discussions, fan theories, and expressions of excitement. Memes, fan art, and speculative posts create a vibrant ecosystem of engagement, reflecting the diverse and passionate fan base that "Gladiator" has cultivated over the years. This online enthusiasm translates into real-world excitement, as fans organize watch parties, create fan fiction, and count down the days to the film's release.

In essence, the anticipation for "Gladiator 2" is a multifaceted phenomenon. It is driven by nostalgia for the original film, curiosity about the new narrative, excitement for the technological advancements, and a deep appreciation for the talent involved. It is a rare blend of emotional resonance and intellectual curiosity, a testament to the power of storytelling to unite and inspire. As the release date draws nearer, the buzz will only grow louder, the excitement more palpable, and the anticipation more intense.

So, dear reader, as you delve into this book and immerse yourself in the world of "Gladiator 2," remember that you are part of a global community, united by a shared love for this epic tale. The journey ahead is filled with secrets, surprises, and everything you need to know about this eagerly awaited blockbuster. Let the countdown begin, and may the anticipation only add to the magic of the cinematic experience that awaits.

Production Background

Development History

In the annals of Hollywood, the making of a film is often as epic as the story it tells. The journey to bring "Gladiator 2" to the screen has been a winding, treacherous road, fraught with challenges and illuminated by moments of creative brilliance. It is a saga that spans years, marked by the relentless pursuit of a vision that seemed almost too grand to realize. To understand the full scope of this endeavor, we must delve deep into the labyrinthine corridors of its development history, where every twist and turn has shaped the film that is now poised to take the world by storm.

Our story begins not in the bustling offices of a modern film studio, but in the echoing halls of cinematic history. The year was 2000, and "Gladiator" had just taken the world by storm. Directed by Ridley Scott and anchored by a powerhouse performance from Russell Crowe, the film was a monumental success. It swept the Academy Awards, winning five Oscars including Best Picture and Best Actor, and grossed over $460 million worldwide. More than that, it rekindled a love for epic historical dramas, setting a new standard for the genre. In the wake of its triumph, whispers of a sequel began to circulate.

However, turning whispers into reality is no simple task. The original "Gladiator" ended on a definitive note, with Maximus Decimus Meridius, the valiant general-turned-gladiator, succumbing to his wounds. His death was a poetic conclusion to a tale of revenge and redemption. How then, could a sequel emerge from such finality? This was the first and perhaps most daunting challenge that faced the filmmakers.

Years passed, and the idea of a sequel to "Gladiator" remained in the realm of speculation and hopeful chatter. Ridley Scott, ever the visionary, occasionally hinted at the possibility, but the narrative hurdles seemed insurmountable. It wasn't until the mid-2010s that the project began to gain real traction.

By then, the cinematic landscape had evolved, and advances in technology offered new possibilities for storytelling. Scott, inspired by the enduring legacy of the original film and buoyed by the advances in CGI and practical effects, began to seriously consider how to return to the world of ancient Rome.

One of the first major milestones in the development of "Gladiator 2" was the involvement of screenwriter Peter Craig. Known for his work on films such as "The Town" and "12 Strong," Craig was brought on board to craft a story that could bridge the gap between the original film and a new narrative. His task was Herculean: to honor the legacy of Maximus while introducing new characters and plotlines that could stand on their own. Craig's approach was both respectful and innovative, seeking to expand the universe of "Gladiator" rather than merely replicate it.

As Craig worked on the script, Ridley Scott assembled a team of producers who shared his passion for the project. Walter F. Parkes and Laurie MacDonald, veterans of the industry with a keen eye for epic storytelling, joined the production. Their experience and vision were instrumental in navigating the complex web of logistics, financing, and creative decisions that such a massive project entails. Together, they formed a nucleus of creative energy that would drive the project forward.

The development process was not without its challenges. One of the most significant was securing the involvement of key cast members. Russell Crowe's Maximus had been the heart and soul of the original film, and his absence loomed large over the sequel. While Crowe's return was highly unlikely given his character's fate, there were discussions about how his presence might still be felt. Flashbacks, spiritual visions, or even a narrative device that allowed Maximus's legacy to influence the new story were all considered.

Another challenge was the sheer scale of the production. "Gladiator 2" was envisioned as a film that would not only match but exceed the grandeur of its predecessor. This meant ambitious set designs, expansive locations, and intricate battle sequences. The logistics of such an undertaking were daunting. Filming in multiple countries, coordinating large casts of extras, and ensuring historical accuracy all required meticulous planning and coordination.

Despite these hurdles, the project continued to gather momentum. By the late 2010s, a script began to take shape that satisfied both the creative team and the studio executives. The story, while rooted in the world of the original "Gladiator," introduced new characters and plotlines that promised to captivate audiences. Central to this new narrative was the character of Lucius, the young boy from the original film, now grown and facing his own set of challenges. This provided a natural bridge between the two films, allowing the sequel to honor the past while forging a new path.

As the script solidified, casting became a primary focus. While the return of certain characters from the original film was met with excitement, the introduction of new faces brought a fresh dynamic to the story. A-list actors and rising stars were considered for various roles, each bringing their unique talents to the table. The casting process was exhaustive, with Ridley Scott personally involved in selecting actors who could embody the complex, multi-dimensional characters envisioned in the script.

Parallel to these developments, the technical aspects of the film were also being meticulously planned. Advances in CGI and practical effects since the original "Gladiator" provided the filmmakers with new tools to create a visually stunning film. The goal was to blend these modern techniques with traditional filmmaking to create a seamless and immersive experience. The production design team, led by Arthur Max, who had worked on the original film, began to conceptualize the sets and locations that would bring ancient Rome to life once more.

One of the most ambitious aspects of the production was the recreation of the Colosseum. While the original film had used a combination of CGI and practical sets, "Gladiator 2" aimed to push the boundaries even further. Detailed models, extensive CGI work, and large-scale practical sets were all employed to create a Colosseum that was both historically accurate and visually breathtaking. The attention to detail was extraordinary, with every aspect of the structure meticulously researched and recreated.

Filming locations were another critical component of the production. To capture the epic scope of the story, the filmmakers scouted locations across Europe and North Africa. From the deserts of Morocco to the rolling hills of Italy, each location was chosen for its ability to convey the grandeur and authenticity of the ancient world. The logistical challenges of filming in multiple countries were immense, but the results promised to be spectacular.

As the project moved into the pre-production phase, the excitement began to build. The combination of a compelling script, a talented cast, and a visionary director promised a film that would live up to the legacy of the original "Gladiator." Behind the scenes, the crew worked tirelessly to bring Ridley Scott's vision to life. Set designs were finalized, costumes were created, and the complex choreography of battle sequences was meticulously planned.

However, as with any major production, unforeseen challenges arose. The global COVID-19 pandemic, which swept across the world in 2020, had a significant impact on the film industry. Filming schedules were disrupted, safety protocols had to be implemented, and the production timeline was pushed back. Despite these setbacks, the determination and resilience of the cast and crew ensured that the project continued to move forward.

By 2023, the production of "Gladiator 2" was in full swing.

Filming commenced, and the first images from the set began to emerge, igniting a fresh wave of excitement among fans and critics. The attention to detail, the scale of the sets, and the performances of the actors all hinted at a film that was poised to be a worthy successor to the original. The challenges faced along the way only added to the sense of accomplishment and anticipation.

In the final stages of production, the focus shifted to post-production. Editing, visual effects, and sound design all played crucial roles in shaping the final product. Hans Zimmer, whose iconic score had been a highlight of the original film, returned to compose the music for the sequel. His involvement was met with widespread approval, and his new compositions promised to evoke the same emotional resonance as the original.

As the release date for "Gladiator 2" approached, the anticipation reached a crescendo. Trailers and promotional materials began to be released, each one carefully crafted to build excitement without giving too much away. The marketing campaign was a masterclass in generating buzz, with strategic releases of information that kept audiences engaged and eager for more.

In conclusion, the development history of "Gladiator 2" is a testament to the dedication, creativity, and perseverance of all those involved. From the initial whispers of a sequel to the grand vision brought to life by Ridley Scott and his team, it is a story of overcoming challenges and pushing the boundaries of what is possible in filmmaking. As audiences around the world prepare to return to the Colosseum, the legacy of "Gladiator" stands as a beacon of excellence and inspiration, guiding the way for a new chapter in this epic saga.

Key Players (Director, Producers, Screenwriters)

In the grand theater of filmmaking, the key players behind the curtain are as crucial as the stars on the screen. They are the architects of dreams, the visionaries who weave together the threads of narrative, emotion, and spectacle into a cohesive tapestry that captivates audiences. "Gladiator 2" is no exception, with a cadre of immensely talented individuals steering the ship. Their collective genius, experience, and passion are the bedrock upon which this epic sequel is built. Let us embark on a journey to explore the minds and hearts of these key players, whose contributions are the lifeblood of "Gladiator 2."

Ridley Scott - The Visionary Director

The name Ridley Scott conjures images of grand vistas, meticulous detail, and stories that linger long after the credits roll. Born in South Shields, England, in 1937, Scott's journey into the world of cinema began with a deep love for visual storytelling. His early work in television and commercials laid the groundwork for a career that would see him become one of the most respected and influential directors of his generation.

Scott's breakthrough came with the 1979 sci-fi horror classic, "Alien," a film that showcased his ability to blend stunning visuals with intense, character-driven narratives. This was followed by "Blade Runner" (1982), a film that has since become a cult classic, praised for its dystopian vision and philosophical depth. But it was "Gladiator" (2000) that truly cemented Scott's legacy. His direction brought ancient Rome to life with such authenticity and emotional resonance that it captivated audiences worldwide and won numerous awards, including the Oscar for Best Picture.

For "Gladiator 2," Scott's role is not just that of a director but a guardian of the original film's legacy. His vision for the sequel is both a continuation and an evolution, aiming to recapture the magic of the first film while exploring new thematic and narrative territories. Scott's meticulous attention to detail, his ability to craft epic scale with intimate emotion, and his unyielding dedication to authenticity are the driving forces behind this highly anticipated sequel.

Walter F. Parkes and Laurie MacDonald - The Veteran Producers

The production duo of Walter F. Parkes and Laurie MacDonald are no strangers to the demands of epic storytelling. Their careers, both individually and collectively, have been marked by a series of high-profile and critically acclaimed films. Parkes, a Yale graduate, began his career as a screenwriter before transitioning into producing. His credits include the Academy Award-winning documentary "The California Reich" (1975) and the blockbuster sci-fi comedy "Men in Black" (1997).

Laurie MacDonald, Parkes' producing partner and spouse, has an equally impressive resume. She began her career in film development at Paramount Pictures before moving into producing. Together, Parkes and MacDonald have produced a string of successful films, including "The Ring" (2002) and "Minority Report" (2002). Their ability to balance commercial success with critical acclaim has made them a formidable force in Hollywood.

For "Gladiator 2," Parkes and MacDonald bring their extensive experience and deep understanding of the filmmaking process. They are the logistical wizards, the ones who ensure that the grand vision of the director is realized without compromise. Their role involves everything from securing financing and managing budgets to overseeing the myriad details of pre-production, production, and post-production. Their collaboration with Ridley Scott is a continuation of a partnership that has already produced cinematic gold, and their shared commitment to storytelling excellence is a cornerstone of "Gladiator 2."

Peter Craig - The Creative Screenwriter

Every epic tale begins with a single word, and in the case

of "Gladiator 2," many of those words come from the pen of Peter Craig. Born into a literary family—his mother is acclaimed novelist Sally Field—Craig's path to screenwriting was paved with the ink of storytelling excellence. He first made his mark with novels, such as "The Martini Shot" (1998) and "Hot Plastic" (2004), before transitioning into screenwriting.

Craig's work as a screenwriter has been marked by a talent for crafting intense, character-driven narratives. His credits include the gripping crime drama "The Town" (2010), co-written with Ben Affleck, and the action-packed "12 Strong" (2018). His ability to blend emotional depth with high-stakes drama made him a perfect fit for the ambitious project of "Gladiator 2."

In crafting the screenplay for "Gladiator 2," Craig faced the daunting task of creating a story that honors the legacy of the original while introducing new characters and plotlines that feel fresh and compelling. His approach has been both respectful and innovative, seeking to expand the universe of "Gladiator" in ways that resonate with contemporary audiences. Craig's narrative craftsmanship is evident in the script's intricate character development, its thematic richness, and its capacity to weave personal stories into the broader epic tapestry.

David Franzoni - The Original Scribe

While Peter Craig is the primary screenwriter for "Gladiator 2," it is important to acknowledge the foundational work of David Franzoni, the original scribe behind "Gladiator." Franzoni, a seasoned screenwriter with a passion for historical epics, brought the story of Maximus Decimus Meridius to life with his script for the 2000 film. His work laid the groundwork for the rich narrative and complex characters that would captivate audiences around the world.

Franzoni's career began with the screenplay for "Jumpin' Jack Flash" (1986), but it was his work on "Amistad" (1997) that truly showcased his talent for historical drama. "Gladiator" was a natural progression, allowing him to explore themes of honor, revenge, and redemption against the backdrop of ancient Rome. While Franzoni is not the primary writer for the sequel, his influence is deeply felt, and his original vision continues to guide the narrative arc of "Gladiator 2."

Hans Zimmer - The Maestro of Emotion

No discussion of the key players behind "Gladiator 2" would be complete without mentioning Hans Zimmer, the legendary composer whose music has become synonymous with the emotional depth and epic scale of the original film. Born in Frankfurt, Germany, Zimmer's journey into the world of music began with synthesizers and electronic music, but his career has spanned a vast array of genres and styles.

Zimmer's score for "Gladiator" is one of the most iconic in film history, blending orchestral power with haunting vocals to create a soundscape that is both timeless and deeply affecting. His collaboration with Lisa Gerrard on the original film produced themes that are instantly recognizable, their melodies evoking the grandeur and pathos of ancient Rome.

For "Gladiator 2," Zimmer returns to compose the score, bringing with him a wealth of experience and a deep emotional connection to the material. His music promises to be a vital component of the film's impact, enhancing the storytelling with themes that resonate on a primal level. Zimmer's ability to capture the essence of a film in his compositions ensures that "Gladiator 2" will be as emotionally stirring as its predecessor.

Arthur Max - The Master of Visual Realism

Arthur Max, the production designer for both "Gladiator" and its sequel, is a maestro of visual storytelling. Born in New York City, Max's career began in the world of architecture and industrial design, but his passion for film led him to the realm of production design. His work is characterized by meticulous attention to detail and an ability to create immersive environments that transport audiences to different times and places.

Max's collaboration with Ridley Scott spans several decades and includes iconic films such as "Black Hawk Down" (2001) and "The Martian" (2015). His work on "Gladiator" was a masterclass in historical recreation, bringing the grandeur of ancient Rome to life with stunning accuracy and artistry. For "Gladiator 2," Max once again delves into the past, using his expertise to craft sets that are both historically authentic and cinematically breathtaking.

Janty Yates - The Costume Virtuoso

Costume design is a crucial element of historical epics, and Janty Yates, the costume designer for "Gladiator" and its sequel, is a true virtuoso in her field. Born in England, Yates began her career in fashion before transitioning to film. Her work is known for its historical accuracy, attention to detail, and ability to enhance character development through clothing.

Yates's costumes for "Gladiator" were instrumental in creating the film's authentic look and feel, from the regal attire of the Roman elite to the rugged armor of the gladiators. For "Gladiator 2," Yates continues her meticulous work, designing costumes that reflect the diverse characters and settings of the story. Her creations are not just garments but integral components of the film's visual narrative.

Conclusion

The journey to bring "Gladiator 2" to life is a collaborative effort, a symphony of talents harmonizing to create something truly extraordinary. From Ridley Scott's visionary direction to Peter Craig's compelling screenplay, from Hans Zimmer's evocative score to Arthur Max's stunning production design, each key player contributes their unique skills and passion to the project. Together, they form a creative force that promises to deliver a sequel worthy of its legendary predecessor. As the sands of the Colosseum await the clash of gladiators once more, the legacy of "Gladiator" continues, guided by these remarkable artists who dare to dream on an epic scale.

Cast and Characters

Returning Cast Members

In the grand tapestry of "Gladiator 2," there are threads woven from the past, characters whose presence echoes through the annals of cinematic history. These returning cast members are the torchbearers of continuity, their stories and performances bridging the gap between the original masterpiece and its much-anticipated sequel. As we prepare to re-enter the world of ancient Rome, let us revisit these familiar faces, understand their significance in the original narrative, and explore the roles they are expected to play in this new chapter.

Connie Nielsen as Lucilla

Connie Nielsen's portrayal of Lucilla in "Gladiator" was nothing short of mesmerizing. Lucilla, the daughter of Emperor Marcus Aurelius and sister to the treacherous Commodus, was a character of immense depth and complexity. Torn between her love for Maximus and her duty to her family, Lucilla navigated a treacherous political landscape with grace and intelligence. Her resilience and determination made her a pivotal figure in the original film.

In "Gladiator 2," Nielsen's return as Lucilla promises to be one of the most significant threads of continuity. As a character who has witnessed the rise and fall of emperors, Lucilla's perspective on the events unfolding in Rome will be invaluable. Her experience and wisdom, tempered by the tragedies she has endured, will likely see her playing a key role in the political dynamics of the sequel. Whether she is guiding a new generation of leaders or maneuvering through the intricacies of power, Lucilla's presence will undoubtedly add depth and gravitas to the narrative.

Djimon Hounsou as Juba

Djimon Hounsou's Juba was a beacon of friendship and loyalty in the brutal world of "Gladiator." A fellow slave and gladiator,

Juba formed a bond with Maximus that transcended the arena. His character embodied the themes of hope and brotherhood, providing emotional resonance amidst the film's violence and intrigue. Juba's final scene, as he buried the figurines of Maximus's family in the Colosseum's sand, was a poignant testament to their bond and his enduring hope for freedom.

Juba's return in "Gladiator 2" is a cause for celebration among fans. His character, marked by strength and integrity, will likely continue to embody the spirit of resilience. In the sequel, we may see Juba in a role that reflects his evolution since the original film. Whether he remains a gladiator or has found a new path, Juba's journey will be integral to the story. His relationships with new and returning characters will provide a rich vein of emotional and narrative depth, reminding us of the enduring human spirit even in the face of adversity.

Derek Jacobi as Senator Gracchus

The esteemed Derek Jacobi brought Senator Gracchus to life with a performance that was both commanding and nuanced. Gracchus, a senator disillusioned with the corruption of Rome under Commodus, was a voice of reason and integrity in the original film. His alliance with Lucilla and his support for Maximus's plan to restore the Republic highlighted his commitment to the ideals of Rome, even as he navigated the dangerous waters of political intrigue.

In "Gladiator 2," Jacobi's Gracchus is expected to continue his role as a stalwart defender of the Republic. His character's political acumen and moral compass will be crucial in the turbulent times that the sequel is set to explore. Gracchus's interactions with other key players, both old and new, will likely shape the political landscape of the film. His return brings with it a sense of continuity and the enduring struggle for a just and honorable Rome.

Spencer Treat Clark as Lucius

In "Gladiator," young Lucius Verus was a symbol of innocence and potential. Played by Spencer Treat Clark, Lucius was the son of Lucilla and the nephew of Commodus. His admiration for Maximus and his brief interactions with the hero hinted at a future filled with promise. Lucius's character represented the possibility of a better future, free from the tyranny of his uncle.

Now, with Clark returning to reprise his role as Lucius, "Gladiator 2" offers an exciting opportunity to see how this character has grown and evolved. As an adult, Lucius may find himself at the center of Rome's political and social upheavals. His upbringing and the influences of his mother and Maximus will shape his actions and decisions. Lucius's journey from innocence to leadership could be one of the central arcs of the sequel, offering a blend of nostalgia and new narrative possibilities.

Expected Dynamics and Interactions

The return of these characters not only provides a sense of continuity but also enriches the narrative tapestry of "Gladiator 2." Their past experiences, relationships, and personal growth will shape their roles in the sequel, creating a complex web of interactions that drive the story forward.

Lucilla and Lucius, mother and son, will likely share a dynamic filled with emotional depth and political intrigue. Their bond, tested by the events of the original film and strengthened by their shared losses, will be crucial as they navigate the new challenges Rome faces. Lucilla's wisdom and Lucius's potential form a potent combination, one that could influence the fate of the empire.

Juba's interactions with Lucius and other new characters will also be significant. As a character who has witnessed the brutality of the arena and the fleeting nature of freedom, Juba's perspective on the unfolding events will be invaluable. His loyalty and strength may inspire others, and his journey towards personal redemption will add a rich emotional layer to the story.

Senator Gracchus's role in the sequel's political landscape cannot be understated. His experience and unwavering commitment to the Republic's ideals will position him as a mentor and strategist, navigating the complex power dynamics that define Rome. His alliances, old and new, will shape the political narrative, providing a bridge between the ideals of the past and the realities of the present.

In conclusion, the return of these beloved characters in "Gladiator 2" is more than just a nostalgic nod to the original film. It is a strategic and narrative choice that enriches the sequel, providing depth, continuity, and emotional resonance. As these characters step back into the world of ancient Rome, they carry with them the weight of their past experiences and the promise of new beginnings. Their journeys, intertwined with those of new characters, will weave a story that honors the legacy of "Gladiator" while forging a path towards an epic future. The sands of the Colosseum await, and with them, the return of heroes and legends.

New Additions to the Cast

As the curtains rise once more on the epic stage of "Gladiator 2," we are greeted not only by familiar faces but also by a cast of new characters, each bringing fresh energy and depth to the unfolding saga. These new additions to the cast promise to enrich the narrative tapestry, weaving their own stories into the grand epic that began over two decades ago. Let us step into the arena and meet these new gladiators of storytelling, understanding their backgrounds, the roles they will play, and how they will fit into the complex world of ancient Rome.

Paul Mescal as Lucius Verus

Leading the charge among the new cast members is Paul Mescal, the Irish actor who has captivated audiences with his breakout role in the critically acclaimed series "Normal People." Mescal's portrayal of Connell Waldron earned him widespread praise for his emotional depth and nuanced performance, showcasing a talent that is both raw and refined. In "Gladiator 2," Mescal takes on the pivotal role of Lucius Verus, the now-grown nephew of Commodus and son of Lucilla.

Lucius, once a symbol of innocence and potential, has grown into a man shaped by the turbulent world around him. Under Mescal's capable hands, Lucius is expected to be a complex character, torn between the ideals of his youth and the harsh realities of political power. As Rome teeters on the edge of chaos, Lucius's journey will be central to the narrative, his choices and actions driving much of the plot. Mescal's ability to convey vulnerability and strength in equal measure makes him the perfect fit for this role, promising a performance that will resonate deeply with audiences.

Barry Keoghan as Sejanus

Barry Keoghan, another rising star from Ireland, joins the cast as Sejanus, a character shrouded in intrigue and ambition. Keoghan's body of work, including standout performances in "Dunkirk" and "The Killing of a Sacred Deer," has established him as an actor capable of delivering intensity and unpredictability. In "Gladiator 2," Sejanus is positioned as a formidable player in the political arena, a man whose ambitions are matched only by his cunning.

Sejanus's character is expected to be a key antagonist, a foil to Lucius and other protagonists. His motivations are complex, driven by a desire for power and influence in a Rome rife with corruption and betrayal. Keoghan's portrayal will likely bring a magnetic and unsettling presence to the screen, capturing the audience's attention with his unique blend of charisma and menace. As Sejanus navigates the treacherous waters of Roman politics, his actions will have far-reaching consequences, shaping the fate of the empire.

Jodie Comer as Julia

British actress Jodie Comer, known for her versatile performances in "Killing Eve" and "The Last Duel," steps into the role of Julia, a character whose intelligence and resourcefulness are her greatest weapons. Comer's ability to inhabit a wide range of characters with depth and authenticity makes her a compelling addition to the cast. In "Gladiator 2," Julia is envisioned as a woman of great influence, possibly a member of the imperial family or a key political figure.

Julia's role in the story is multifaceted. She is a strategist, a diplomat, and perhaps a manipulator, using her wits to navigate the dangerous corridors of power. Her interactions with Lucius, Sejanus, and other characters will be pivotal, as she balances her ambitions with her personal loyalties and desires. Comer's portrayal promises to bring a dynamic and layered performance to the film, adding a powerful female presence to the epic narrative.

Joseph Quinn as Marcellus

Joseph Quinn, who gained recognition for his role as Eddie Munson in "Stranger Things," joins the cast as Marcellus, a character whose background and motivations are closely tied to the central conflict of the film. Quinn's ability to bring charm and complexity to his roles makes him an exciting addition to "Gladiator 2." Marcellus is expected to be a character with a mysterious past and uncertain allegiances, adding an element of unpredictability to the story.

Marcellus's journey will likely intersect with those of Lucius, Sejanus, and Julia, creating a web of relationships that drive the plot forward. His actions and decisions will play a crucial role in the unfolding drama, as he navigates the blurred lines between friend and foe. Quinn's performance is anticipated to bring depth and nuance to Marcellus, making him a character to watch as the story progresses.

John David Washington as Marcus

John David Washington, celebrated for his roles in "BlacKkKlansman" and "Tenet," brings his formidable talent to the role of Marcus, a new character whose presence in "Gladiator 2" promises to be significant. Washington's powerful screen presence and ability to convey both physical prowess and emotional complexity make him an ideal fit for the world of ancient Rome. Marcus is envisioned as a warrior, perhaps a gladiator or a soldier, whose path intersects with Lucius and the other main characters.

Marcus's role in the story is expected to be one of action and honor, a character driven by a code of ethics in a world where such values are often compromised. Washington's portrayal will likely bring a sense of gravitas and intensity to Marcus, making him a pivotal figure in the film's epic battles and personal conflicts. His journey will add a layer of heroism and struggle to the narrative, enriching the overall tapestry of the story.

Fitting into the Story

The integration of these new characters into the world of "Gladiator 2" is a delicate and deliberate process, one that aims to expand the narrative while maintaining continuity with the original film. Each character brings with them a unique set of motivations, backgrounds, and conflicts, creating a rich and dynamic ensemble that promises to captivate audiences.

Lucius Verus, under Paul Mescal's portrayal, is the central thread connecting the past to the present. His journey from innocence to leadership mirrors the broader themes of the film, exploring the burdens of power and the quest for justice in a corrupted world. Lucius's interactions with characters like Sejanus, Julia, Marcellus, and Marcus will be crucial in shaping the story, each relationship adding layers of intrigue, conflict, and emotional depth.

Sejanus, played by Barry Keoghan, serves as a dark mirror to Lucius's idealism, his ambitions and machinations driving much of the political drama. Jodie Comer's Julia, with her intelligence and strategic acumen, will navigate these treacherous waters, her alliances and rivalries adding complexity to the narrative. Joseph Quinn's Marcellus, with his mysterious past, introduces an element of unpredictability, while John David Washington's Marcus brings a sense of honor and heroism to the story's epic scale.

Together, these new additions to the cast of "Gladiator 2" promise to create a rich, multifaceted narrative that honors the legacy of the original while forging a path towards new and exciting storytelling horizons. As the dust settles in the Colosseum and the echoes of battle fade, these characters will leave their mark on the epic saga, their stories intertwining with those of the past and shaping the future of ancient Rome.

Character Profiles and Predictions

As we step into the grand arena of "Gladiator 2," we are greeted by a cast of characters, each with their own intricate backgrounds, motivations, and potential arcs. These characters, both returning and new, weave a rich tapestry that promises to enthrall audiences with their complex interplay of ambition, honor, and destiny. Let us delve into their profiles, exploring their pasts, their driving forces, and the paths they might tread in this highly anticipated sequel.

Lucius Verus (Paul Mescal)

Background: Lucius Verus, the son of Lucilla and nephew of the nefarious Commodus, was once a boy who idolized the heroic Maximus Decimus Meridius. Growing up amidst the turmoil and bloodshed of Rome's political machinations, Lucius has now matured into a young man, shaped by the shadow of his family's legacy and the heroics of Maximus. His experiences have instilled in him a deep sense of justice, but also a keen awareness of the treacherous landscape he must navigate.

Motivations: Lucius is driven by a desire to restore honor to his family's name and to Rome itself. Haunted by the memory of Maximus, he seeks to uphold the principles of bravery, loyalty, and righteousness that the fallen gladiator embodied. Lucius is also motivated by the need to protect his mother, Lucilla, and to secure a future where Rome can thrive free from corruption and tyranny.

Predicted Arc: In "Gladiator 2," Lucius's journey will likely center around his struggle to balance idealism with the harsh realities of power. As he steps into a leadership role, he will face formidable enemies and moral dilemmas that test his convictions. His interactions with other key characters, such as Sejanus and Julia, will shape his development, as he learns the complexities of governance and the sacrifices required to achieve true justice. Lucius's arc may culminate in a defining moment where he must choose between vengeance and mercy, echoing the internal conflicts that once tormented Maximus.

Sejanus (Barry Keoghan)

Background: Sejanus emerges as a formidable and enigmatic figure in the world of "Gladiator 2." Little is known about his origins, but his rise through the ranks of Roman society speaks to his cunning and ambition. He is a man who has navigated the treacherous waters of Roman politics with ruthless efficiency, always staying one step ahead of his adversaries.

Motivations: Sejanus is driven by an insatiable thirst for power and control. Unlike Lucius, whose motivations are rooted in honor, Sejanus's ambitions are purely self-serving. He views the political arena as a game, one in which he is determined to emerge victorious, regardless of the cost. His manipulation and strategic alliances are tools he wields with precision, always with an eye towards consolidating his influence.

Predicted Arc: Sejanus is poised to be a primary antagonist in "Gladiator 2," a shadowy figure whose machinations challenge Lucius at every turn. His arc will likely involve a series of power plays and betrayals, as he seeks to undermine Lucius's efforts to reform Rome. Sejanus's downfall, when it comes, will be a spectacle of poetic justice, perhaps engineered through the very machinations he used to climb to power. His interactions with Julia and other political figures will add layers of intrigue and danger to the narrative.

Julia (Jodie Comer)

Background: Julia is a character of sophistication and intellect, potentially a member of the imperial family or a high-ranking political figure. Her upbringing in the elite circles of Roman society has endowed her with a sharp mind and a keen understanding of the power dynamics at play. She is a woman who knows how to navigate the corridors of power with grace and strategy.

Motivations: Julia's motivations are multifaceted. On one hand, she seeks to maintain her own position and influence within the empire. On the other, she is driven by a genuine desire to see Rome thrive and prosper. Her actions are guided by a blend of personal ambition and a vision for a greater good, making her both an ally and a potential adversary to those around her.

Predicted Arc: Julia's role in "Gladiator 2" will be one of complexity and duality. Her relationship with Lucius could evolve into a partnership grounded in mutual respect and shared goals, though not without its tensions. Julia may also find herself at odds with Sejanus, their ambitions clashing in a high-stakes game of political chess. Her character arc will likely explore themes of loyalty, sacrifice, and the cost of power, as she navigates her place in a changing Rome.

Marcellus (Joseph Quinn)

Background: Marcellus is a character cloaked in mystery, with a past that is hinted at but not fully revealed. His journey has taken him through various roles—perhaps a soldier, a gladiator, or a rogue—each shaping his outlook and skills. Marcellus is a survivor, someone who has learned to adapt and thrive in the harshest of environments.

Motivations: Marcellus is driven by a need to find his place in the world and to reconcile his past with his future. He is searching for a sense of purpose and belonging, something that has eluded him throughout his tumultuous life. His motivations are deeply personal, tied to a desire for redemption and meaning.

Predicted Arc: In "Gladiator 2," Marcellus's journey will likely intertwine with those of Lucius and other central characters. His past experiences will provide valuable insights and skills that aid in their collective struggles. Marcellus's arc may involve uncovering hidden truths about his own identity and purpose, culminating in a moment of self-discovery and resolution. His character will add depth and humanity to the narrative, reflecting the broader themes of identity and destiny.

Marcus (John David Washington)

Background: Marcus is envisioned as a warrior, possibly a former gladiator or a soldier with a storied past. His experiences on the battlefield have forged him into a formidable force, both physically and mentally. Marcus's background is marked by hardship and struggle, shaping him into a man of principle and honor.

Motivations: Marcus is motivated by a code of ethics and a desire to uphold justice. He is a character who values honor above all else, and his actions are guided by a deep sense of duty. Marcus's loyalty is hard-won but unwavering, making him a steadfast ally and a formidable opponent.

Predicted Arc: In "Gladiator 2," Marcus's role will likely involve serving as a mentor and protector to Lucius and others. His wisdom and experience will be invaluable in navigating the perils they face. Marcus's arc may explore themes of redemption, as he seeks to atone for past actions and find peace with his own conscience. His journey will add a layer of heroism and nobility to the story, highlighting the enduring power of honor and integrity.

Interwoven Arcs and Relationships

The interplay between these characters will be the heartbeat of "Gladiator 2," driving the narrative forward with their intersecting paths and conflicting ambitions. Lucius and Sejanus will represent the classic struggle between idealism and ambition, their interactions charged with tension and stakes that ripple through the entire plot. Julia's strategic mind and political acumen will place her at the center of many pivotal moments, her alliances and rivalries shaping the course of events.

Marcellus and Marcus, with their rich backstories and personal quests, will bring depth and humanity to the epic scale of the narrative. Their relationships with the other characters will be marked by moments of camaraderie, conflict, and profound realization, each adding a unique thread to the story's intricate tapestry.

As "Gladiator 2" unfolds, these characters will navigate a world filled with danger, intrigue, and the ever-present specter of destiny. Their arcs, both individual and collective, will explore the timeless themes of power, honor, and the search for identity. Together, they will forge a new chapter in the saga of ancient Rome, one that promises to captivate and inspire audiences with its depth, complexity, and enduring human spirit.

Plot and Storyline
Overview of Gladiator (2000) Plot

Once upon a time, in the waning days of the Roman Empire, a tale of betrayal, vengeance, and redemption unfolded on the silver screen, captivating audiences with its grandeur and emotional depth. Ridley Scott's "Gladiator," released in 2000, is a sweeping epic that tells the story of Maximus Decimus Meridius, a revered Roman general who falls from grace only to rise again as a gladiator seeking justice. The film is a masterful blend of historical drama and personal tragedy, woven together with themes of honor, loyalty, and the undying human spirit.

The story begins on the cold, windswept plains of Germania, where Maximus, played by the formidable Russell Crowe, leads the Roman army to a decisive victory against a barbarian horde. His prowess on the battlefield and his unwavering loyalty to Emperor Marcus Aurelius have earned him the admiration of his troops and the trust of the aging emperor. Marcus Aurelius, portrayed by the venerable Richard Harris, is a philosopher-king, wise and weary, who dreams of restoring the Republic and ending the corrupt rule of the Caesars.

In a moment of quiet reflection, Marcus Aurelius reveals to Maximus his plan to name him as his successor, bypassing his own son, Commodus. The emperor sees in Maximus the virtues that he believes Rome desperately needs—integrity, courage, and a sense of duty. Maximus, loyal to a fault, is reluctant but agrees to serve Rome as its protector.

However, the emperor's intentions are not to be realized. Commodus, played with chilling intensity by Joaquin Phoenix, learns of his father's plans and, in a fit of rage and desperation, murders Marcus Aurelius. The young, ambitious, and deeply insecure Commodus seizes power, declaring himself emperor. He commands the arrest of Maximus and orders his execution. Betrayed and heartbroken, Maximus escapes his executioners, but not in time to save his family from Commodus's wrath. His wife and son are brutally murdered, their farm burned to the ground.

Maximus, wounded and grief-stricken, is captured by slave traders and sold to Proximo, a gladiator trainer played by the late Oliver Reed in a powerful performance. In the dusty, blood-soaked arenas of North Africa, Maximus is reborn as a gladiator, a shadow of his former self but with a fire of vengeance burning in his heart. Under Proximo's tutelage, he rises through the ranks, his skill and ferocity in the arena earning him the moniker "The Spaniard."

Meanwhile, in Rome, Commodus's rule is marked by excess and cruelty. He seeks to win the favor of the people through lavish games and spectacles, all the while tightening his grip on power. His sister, Lucilla, played with grace and strength by Connie Nielsen, is trapped in a web of fear and manipulation. She navigates the dangerous politics of the imperial court, torn between her love for her son, Lucius, and her desire to see Commodus overthrown.

Fate brings Maximus to Rome, where he is to fight in the Colosseum, the grandest arena of them all. His prowess as a gladiator captures the imagination of the Roman populace, and he becomes a symbol of hope and defiance against Commodus's tyranny. In a stunning display of courage and skill, Maximus leads his fellow gladiators to victory in a series of spectacular battles, each one more thrilling and perilous than the last.

Maximus's identity is eventually revealed to the astonished crowd and the horrified Commodus. The emperor, seething with jealousy and rage, confronts Maximus in the arena but is unable to kill him outright without inciting the wrath of the people. Instead, he plots to undermine Maximus's growing influence by challenging him to a rigged duel. Commodus, a skilled but unscrupulous fighter, wounds Maximus beforehand, ensuring his victory.

The final confrontation between Maximus and Commodus is

a heart-pounding climax. Despite his injuries, Maximus fights with the strength of a man who has nothing left to lose. The duel is brutal and bloody, a testament to the resilience and tenacity of Maximus's spirit. In a moment of poetic justice, Maximus overcomes Commodus, plunging a dagger into his throat. With his dying breath, Maximus secures the release of his fellow gladiators and orders the restoration of the Republic, fulfilling the wish of Marcus Aurelius.

Maximus, mortally wounded, collapses onto the sands of the Colosseum. His life's journey, marked by tragedy and triumph, comes to an end as he is reunited with his slain wife and son in the afterlife. His death is both a release and a victory, a poignant conclusion to his relentless quest for justice and redemption.

The film closes with Lucilla, Lucius, and the senator Gracchus paying tribute to Maximus. His legacy, one of honor, bravery, and unwavering loyalty, endures. He is remembered as a hero who fought not for glory or power but for the soul of Rome itself.

"Gladiator" is more than just a tale of revenge and redemption; it is a meditation on the nature of power, the corrupting influence of ambition, and the enduring strength of the human spirit. Ridley Scott's direction, combined with Hans Zimmer's haunting score and John Mathieson's breathtaking cinematography, creates a film that is as visually stunning as it is emotionally profound.

As we prepare for the arrival of "Gladiator 2," the legacy of the original film looms large. Maximus's story has set the stage for a new chapter, one that promises to explore the aftermath of his heroic sacrifice and the continuing struggle for Rome's soul. The themes of honor, loyalty, and the fight against tyranny are timeless, resonating as powerfully today as they did two decades ago. The sands of the Colosseum may have settled, but the echoes of Maximus Decimus Meridius's defiant cry—"Are you not entertained?"—still reverberate, challenging us to confront our own battles with courage and integrity.

Confirmed Plot Details for Gladiator 2

As the world eagerly awaits the return to the grandeur of ancient Rome, "Gladiator 2" promises to transport audiences back to the blood-soaked sands of the Colosseum, into a tale woven with the threads of legacy, power, and redemption. The sequel, directed once more by Ridley Scott, aims to build on the monumental success of the original film, exploring new narratives while honoring the characters and themes that captivated audiences two decades ago. Here, we delve into the confirmed plot details, key events, and character arcs that will shape this epic continuation.

The Setting

"Gladiator 2" picks up years after the death of Maximus Decimus Meridius. The Roman Empire, still vast and powerful, is at a crossroads. Commodus's tyrannical reign has left scars on the empire, and the shadow of his rule still lingers. However, the people's spirit remains unbroken, and there is a yearning for a return to the values of honor and justice that Maximus represented. This sequel promises to explore a Rome that is both familiar and changed, where old enemies and new alliances emerge in the struggle for power.

Lucius Verus: The Prodigal Son

At the heart of "Gladiator 2" is Lucius Verus, portrayed by Paul Mescal. Lucius, once a boy who looked up to Maximus as a hero, is now a man ready to carve out his destiny. Raised under the protective and watchful eye of his mother, Lucilla, Lucius has grown into a figure of both potential and uncertainty. He carries the weight of his family's legacy and the expectations of those who see in him the promise of a better future for Rome.

Lucius's journey is one of self-discovery and leadership. Haunted by the memories of his uncle Commodus and inspired by the heroics of Maximus, he seeks to restore honor to the empire. His arc will see him navigating the treacherous waters of Roman politics, facing challenges that test his resolve and character. Lucius's transformation from a young nobleman to a leader who can unify a fractured Rome is central to the film's narrative.

The Rise of Sejanus

Opposing Lucius is the cunning and ambitious Sejanus, played by Barry Keoghan. Sejanus is a man of shadows, operating within the intricate and dangerous web of Roman politics. He is a master manipulator, driven by an insatiable thirst for power and control. His rise to prominence has been marked by strategic alliances and ruthless decisions, positioning him as a formidable adversary to Lucius.

Sejanus's character adds a layer of intrigue and tension to the storyline. His motivations are complex, rooted in a desire to dominate the political landscape of Rome. As he vies for power, Sejanus employs tactics that range from cunning diplomacy to outright treachery. His interactions with other characters, particularly Lucius and Julia, create a dynamic interplay of alliances and rivalries that drive the plot forward.

Julia: The Strategist

Jodie Comer takes on the role of Julia, a character of intelligence and influence. Julia's background in the elite circles of Roman society has honed her skills in strategy and politics. She is a woman who understands the power of subtlety and the importance of alliances. Her motivations are multifaceted, blending personal ambition with a genuine desire to see Rome flourish.

Julia's role in "Gladiator 2" is pivotal. She acts as both an ally and a counterbalance to Lucius, guiding him through the complexities of leadership while also pursuing her own goals. Her relationship with Sejanus is one of careful navigation, each step a calculated move in the broader game of power. Julia's arc explores themes of loyalty, sacrifice, and the fine line between manipulation and genuine care.

Marcellus: The Enigma

Joseph Quinn's Marcellus is a character shrouded in mystery. His past is a mosaic of battles fought and lost, a tapestry of experiences that have shaped him into a warrior of remarkable skill and resilience. Marcellus's motivations are deeply personal, tied to a quest for redemption and a search for identity.

In "Gladiator 2," Marcellus's journey intersects with those of Lucius, Sejanus, and Julia. His character adds depth and unpredictability to the narrative, as his actions are driven by a blend of loyalty and self-interest. Marcellus's arc is one of transformation, as he grapples with his past and seeks to forge a new path. His evolution from a solitary figure to a key player in Rome's future is a testament to the film's exploration of redemption and personal growth.

Marcus: The Protector

John David Washington steps into the role of Marcus, a character defined by his sense of duty and honor. Marcus's background as a soldier or former gladiator has endowed him with a strong moral compass and an unwavering commitment to justice. His motivations are clear and noble, driven by a desire to uphold the values that Rome once stood for.

Marcus's role in the sequel is that of a mentor and protector. He provides guidance to Lucius and serves as a stabilizing force amidst the chaos. His character embodies the virtues of bravery and integrity, and his journey is one of leading by example. Marcus's interactions with other characters highlight the importance of mentorship and the enduring impact of moral leadership.

Key Events and Themes

The narrative of "Gladiator 2" is woven with key events that reflect the grand scale and emotional depth of its predecessor. The film promises to delve into the intricacies of Roman politics, the brutal realities of power struggles, and the personal journeys of its characters.

1. **The Quest for Unity:** Lucius's primary goal is to unify Rome under a banner of honor and justice. This quest is fraught with obstacles, from internal dissent to external threats. The film explores his efforts to build alliances, earn the trust of the people, and confront those who seek to undermine his vision.

2. **Political Intrigue:** Sejanus's machinations add a layer of suspense and tension to the storyline. His maneuvers in the political arena create a chess game of power, where each move has far-reaching consequences. The interplay between Sejanus and other key characters, particularly Lucius and Julia, is a driving force of the plot.

3. **Personal Redemption:** Marcellus's journey towards redemption is a poignant subplot. His interactions with Lucius and Marcus help him confront his past and find a new sense of purpose. This theme of personal growth and transformation adds emotional depth to the narrative.

4. **The Role of Women:** Julia's character highlights the significant role women play in shaping the future of Rome. Her strategic mind and influence are crucial to the unfolding events, and her relationship with Lucius underscores the importance of partnership and mutual respect.

5. **The Shadow of Maximus:** The legacy of Maximus looms large over the sequel. His values and heroics serve as a guiding light for Lucius, and his memory is a source of inspiration and pressure. The film pays homage to Maximus's impact while forging a new path for its characters.

6. **Epic Battles:** True to its predecessor, "Gladiator 2" features grand and visceral battle scenes. These

confrontations are not only spectacles of action but also pivotal moments of character development and narrative progression. The choreography and scale of these battles promise to be as breathtaking as they are integral to the story.

7. **Themes of Power and Integrity:** The film delves into the nature of power and the moral choices that come with it. Characters like Lucius and Marcus represent the struggle to wield power responsibly, while Sejanus embodies the dangers of unchecked ambition. This exploration of ethics and governance is a central theme.

Conclusion

"Gladiator 2" is set to be an epic continuation of a beloved story, filled with complex characters, grand ambitions, and a richly textured narrative. As we prepare to return to the world of ancient Rome, the confirmed plot details reveal a film that honors its predecessor while boldly charting new territory. Lucius Verus's journey from a boy in the shadow of heroes to a leader in his own right promises to be a compelling and emotional arc. The interplay of political intrigue, personal redemption, and the enduring fight for honor ensures that "Gladiator 2" will be a worthy successor to the original, capturing the imagination and hearts of audiences once more.

Speculations and Fan Theories

As anticipation for "Gladiator 2" reaches fever pitch, the internet is abuzz with speculations and fan theories. These predictions range from the plausible to the fantastical, each adding a layer of intrigue and excitement to the unfolding narrative. The enigmatic whispers of what might be have captured the imaginations of fans and critics alike, each theory a testament to the enduring legacy of the original film. Let us dive into this rich tapestry of speculation, exploring the myriad possibilities that have ignited the collective imagination.

The Return of Maximus

Perhaps the most persistent and tantalizing theory revolves around the potential return of Maximus Decimus Meridius. Despite his poignant death in the original film, fans have speculated on various ways his character could make a comeback. One popular theory suggests a supernatural element, where Maximus might return as a ghost or a guiding spirit. This ethereal presence could offer counsel to Lucius, echoing the timeless theme of legacy and the enduring influence of the past.

Another theory posits that Maximus might be resurrected through a dramatic twist of fate or ancient Roman magic, a concept not entirely out of place in the mythological context of ancient Rome. While this might seem far-fetched, it has captured the imaginations of fans who long to see Russell Crowe's iconic character once more. Even a series of flashbacks or dream sequences could serve to keep Maximus's presence alive, providing poignant moments of reflection and motivation for Lucius.

The Role of Lucius

As the confirmed protagonist of "Gladiator 2," Lucius Verus is at the center of numerous fan theories. One of the most compelling ideas is that Lucius will struggle with the darker aspects of power, mirroring the internal conflict that Maximus faced. Raised in the shadow of both his uncle Commodus and the heroic Maximus, Lucius's journey might involve a battle against his own demons, perhaps even grappling with a thirst for revenge or a desire for unchecked power.

Some fans speculate that Lucius will have to confront hidden truths about his lineage. Could there be a revelation about his true parentage that shakes the very foundations of his identity? Such a twist would add a layer of complexity to his character, driving his actions and decisions in unexpected ways. The theory that Lucius might discover a direct connection to Maximus, whether through blood or spiritual kinship, has been floated by those who seek a deeper intertwining of their fates.

Sejanus's Ambition

Barry Keoghan's Sejanus has sparked a flurry of theories, primarily focused on his ambitions and ultimate goals. Fans predict that Sejanus will not only challenge Lucius for power but will do so with a Machiavellian flair that rivals Commodus's treachery. The theory that Sejanus might manipulate the Senate and the Praetorian Guard to stage a coup is a popular one, suggesting a high-stakes game of political chess where every move could determine the fate of the empire.

Another intriguing speculation is that Sejanus might seek to exploit Rome's enemies to further his own power. This could involve secret alliances with foreign powers or even instigating conflicts that he can then use to his advantage. Such actions would paint him as a master strategist, a puppet master pulling the strings from behind the scenes. His interactions with Julia and other key figures would be fraught with tension and deception, each alliance a potential betrayal in the making.

Julia's Duality

Julia, portrayed by Jodie Comer, is a character shrouded in complexity, and fan theories reflect this. One prevalent theory is that Julia will act as both an ally and an antagonist to Lucius, her motivations a blend of personal ambition and genuine care for Rome's future. Some fans speculate that Julia might initially support Sejanus's rise, believing it to be the best path for stability, only to switch allegiances as his true nature is revealed.

There is also the theory that Julia's character will embody the ancient Roman archetype of the cunning and influential woman. She might use her intellect and charm to navigate the treacherous waters of Roman politics, playing various factions against each other to secure her own power. Her potential romantic entanglement with Lucius or even Sejanus is another point of speculation, adding layers of personal conflict and drama to her arc.

Marcellus's Mysteries

Joseph Quinn's Marcellus remains one of the most enigmatic characters, fueling a variety of theories about his true purpose and background. One theory suggests that Marcellus might be a former ally or enemy of Maximus, returning to Rome with a personal vendetta or a debt to repay. His character could serve as a link to Maximus's past, revealing hidden facets of the hero's life and legacy.

Another popular idea is that Marcellus could be a spy or double agent, working for Sejanus or a foreign power. His motivations might be hidden beneath layers of deception, making him a wild card in the unfolding drama. Fans also speculate that Marcellus might have a deeply personal quest for redemption, his journey paralleling that of Lucius in surprising and meaningful ways.

The Shadow of Maximus

The legacy of Maximus is a recurring theme in many fan theories, with some speculating that his influence will be felt through relics, messages, or hidden teachings discovered by Lucius. There is a poignant theory that Maximus might have left behind a secret order or group of followers dedicated to his ideals, who now seek to support Lucius in his quest to restore honor to Rome.

This could manifest in the form of hidden scrolls or artifacts that Lucius uncovers, each one providing guidance and wisdom. Alternatively, Lucius might encounter old comrades of Maximus who offer their support, their loyalty to the fallen hero now transferred to his protégé. Such elements would serve to bridge the past and present, creating a rich tapestry of continuity and homage.

The Spiritual and Mythological

Some of the more fantastical theories delve into the spiritual and mythological aspects of the Roman world. There are speculations that "Gladiator 2" might incorporate elements of Roman mythology, with gods and supernatural forces playing a role in the narrative. Lucius could be portrayed as a chosen figure, his destiny intertwined with the will of the gods, adding a layer of epic grandeur to his journey.

One particularly imaginative theory suggests that Lucius might undertake a quest reminiscent of the classical hero's journey, facing trials and challenges set by the gods themselves. This could involve visions, prophetic dreams, or encounters with mythical creatures, blending historical drama with mythological fantasy. Such an approach would elevate the story to a new level of epic storytelling, resonating with the timeless myths that have captivated humanity for millennia.

The Role of Marcus

John David Washington's Marcus is also a focal point for fan theories, with many predicting that his character will serve as a mentor and protector to Lucius. Some speculate that Marcus might be a former gladiator or soldier who once fought alongside or against Maximus, now seeking redemption through his alliance with Lucius. His character's arc could explore themes of loyalty, sacrifice, and the enduring struggle for justice.

There is also the theory that Marcus might have a personal vendetta against Sejanus, adding another layer of conflict to the narrative. His motivations could be driven by a desire to avenge past wrongs or to prevent Sejanus from repeating the atrocities of Commodus's reign. Marcus's role as a moral compass and warrior would provide a strong counterbalance to the political intrigue and personal dramas unfolding in the story.

The Future of Rome

Ultimately, many fan theories converge on the broader theme of Rome's future. Will Lucius succeed in restoring the Republic and the values it once stood for, or will the empire descend further into tyranny and chaos? Some fans predict a bittersweet ending, where Lucius's efforts bring about change but at a great personal cost. Others envision a triumphant conclusion, with Lucius emerging as a new kind of leader who blends the best of the old and new worlds.

There are also darker theories that suggest a tragic end, with Lucius falling victim to the same forces that claimed Maximus, leaving Rome's fate uncertain. This would serve as a stark commentary on the cyclical nature of power and corruption, reflecting the complexities of human nature and governance. Whether the ending is hopeful or tragic, the journey promises to be one of profound emotional and philosophical depth.

Conclusion

The speculations and fan theories surrounding "Gladiator 2" are as varied and rich as the world of ancient Rome itself. They reflect a deep engagement with the characters, themes, and narrative possibilities introduced by the original film. As we await the sequel's release, these theories fuel the imagination, each one a potential pathway through the labyrinthine corridors of power, honor, and destiny. Whether grounded in historical realism or soaring into mythological fantasy, they all share a common thread: the enduring fascination with a story that continues to resonate across the ages.

Filming Locations and Production Design

Primary Filming Locations

In the realm of filmmaking, the canvas upon which a story is painted is as vital as the tale itself. For "Gladiator 2," the selection of filming locations has been a meticulous process, aimed at capturing the grandeur and authenticity of ancient Rome. Each location serves as a portal, transporting the audience back to a time of emperors and gladiators, of vast arenas and bustling cities. Let us embark on a journey through the primary filming locations of this epic sequel, exploring their significance and the unique contributions they bring to the film's setting.

Morocco: The Timeless Sands

Morocco, with its sweeping deserts and ancient cities, has long been a favorite for filmmakers seeking to capture the mystique and majesty of ancient worlds. For "Gladiator 2," the Moroccan landscapes once again provide a backdrop that evokes the harsh beauty and unforgiving nature of the gladiatorial life. The country's vast, rolling dunes and rugged terrain serve as stand-ins for the North African provinces of the Roman Empire, where Maximus once fought and where new battles will be waged.

In the heart of Morocco, the city of Ouarzazate, often dubbed the "Gateway to the Desert," plays a pivotal role. Known for its film studios and historic kasbahs, Ouarzazate offers a blend of authenticity and accessibility. The city's architecture, with its mud-brick buildings and labyrinthine streets, provides a perfect canvas for the bustling markets and chaotic arenas of the ancient world. The nearby Atlas Mountains add a dramatic backdrop, their peaks and valleys echoing the epic scale of the story.

The sands of Morocco are not just a visual spectacle but a character in their own right, representing the relentless challenges faced by the film's protagonists. The harsh desert climate and stark beauty underscore the themes of endurance and survival that are central to "Gladiator 2."

Italy: The Heart of Rome

No film set in the Roman Empire would be complete without scenes shot in Italy, the cradle of Roman civilization. For "Gladiator 2," Italy's historic cities and landscapes provide an irreplaceable authenticity. Rome, with its iconic ruins and timeless beauty, serves as both a symbol and a setting. The ancient Colosseum, although largely reconstructed through CGI and practical effects, is grounded in the real Rome, where the echoes of gladiators still seem to linger in the stones.

One of the standout locations is the Cinecittà Studios in Rome. Known as the hub of Italian cinema, Cinecittà has hosted countless historical epics. For "Gladiator 2," the studios offer state-of-the-art facilities combined with a rich cinematic history. Here, detailed sets recreate the grandeur of Roman architecture, from the opulent palaces of the elite to the grimy backstreets where conspiracies brew. The meticulous attention to detail in the set design ensures that every stone, column, and archway contributes to an immersive experience.

Additionally, the city of Florence, with its Renaissance architecture and rich history, provides a stunning backdrop for scenes that require a blend of urban grandeur and intimate moments. The Ponte Vecchio, the Uffizi Gallery, and the winding streets of the historic center bring to life the vibrant, complex society of ancient Rome.

Malta: The Island Fortress

Malta, a jewel in the Mediterranean, reprises its role as a key location for "Gladiator 2." The island's ancient fortifications and coastal landscapes offer a versatile setting for various scenes. Valletta, Malta's capital, with its imposing bastions and baroque architecture, stands in for parts of the Roman Empire's frontier towns and military outposts. The city's historic streets and harbors evoke a sense of timelessness, seamlessly blending with the film's period setting.

The island's rugged coastlines and azure waters also provide the perfect backdrop for naval scenes and coastal battles. The ancient city of Mdina, with its narrow, winding streets and medieval charm, doubles as both Roman cities and provincial towns. The limestone buildings, bathed in the Mediterranean sun, add a layer of authenticity and visual splendor.

Malta's role in "Gladiator 2" is not just about aesthetics; it is about capturing the strategic and cultural crossroads that defined the Roman Empire. The island's blend of natural beauty and historic architecture creates a vivid, immersive world where the story can unfold with all its intended grandeur.

Spain: The Empire's Breadbasket

Spain's diverse landscapes have long been a draw for filmmakers, offering everything from rolling plains to dramatic mountains. For "Gladiator 2," Spain provides a setting that captures the agricultural heartland and the distant provinces of the Roman Empire. The region of Andalusia, with its sun-drenched fields and ancient olive groves, stands in for the empire's fertile territories.

The historic city of Seville, with its mix of Roman, Moorish, and Renaissance architecture, offers a rich tapestry for the film's urban scenes. The Alcázar of Seville, with its intricate gardens and palatial rooms, doubles as the luxurious residences of Roman elites and the intricate political intrigues of the Senate. The blend of architectural styles in Seville mirrors the cultural melting pot that was ancient Rome.

In addition, the rugged terrain of the Sierra Nevada mountains and the expansive plains of Castilla-La Mancha provide a versatile backdrop for battle scenes and the journeys of the film's characters. The stark contrast between Spain's lush agricultural areas and its harsh, mountainous regions underscores the diversity and reach of the Roman Empire.

The United Kingdom: The Distant Frontier

The windswept moors and ancient woodlands of the United

Kingdom offer a stark, dramatic contrast to the sun-drenched locales of the Mediterranean. For "Gladiator 2," the UK serves as the empire's distant frontiers, where the might of Rome clashes with the untamed wilderness. The Scottish Highlands, with their rugged beauty and haunting landscapes, provide the perfect setting for scenes depicting the northernmost reaches of the empire.

Hadrian's Wall, a symbol of Roman engineering and ambition, plays a significant role in the film. The ancient fortifications and surrounding countryside evoke the constant tension between Rome and the barbarian tribes. The wall's presence serves as a reminder of the empire's limits and the ever-present threat beyond its borders.

The ancient forests of England, particularly in regions like Sherwood Forest and the New Forest, offer a lush, green contrast to the arid deserts and bustling cities. These woodlands are used for scenes of intrigue and refuge, where characters might hide from their pursuers or plot their next move away from the prying eyes of the Roman authorities.

Conclusion

The primary filming locations for "Gladiator 2" are more than just backdrops; they are integral components of the film's storytelling. Each location, from the timeless sands of Morocco to the historic streets of Rome, adds depth and authenticity to the narrative. The careful selection of these sites reflects a commitment to capturing the grandeur and complexity of the Roman Empire, immersing audiences in a world where history and fiction blend seamlessly.

These locations, with their unique landscapes and rich histories, serve to transport viewers back to an era of epic battles, political intrigue, and personal redemption. They are the stage upon which the drama of "Gladiator 2" unfolds, each one contributing to the visual and emotional tapestry of the film. As the story of Lucius Verus and his struggle for Rome's soul is brought to life, these filming locations ensure that the legacy of "Gladiator" continues to resonate with power and authenticity.

Set Design and Aesthetic Choices

In the world of "Gladiator 2," the set design and aesthetic choices are not merely backdrops but integral to the storytelling, creating a vivid and immersive experience that transports audiences back to the grandeur and brutality of ancient Rome. The visual splendor, intricate details, and thematic coherence of the set designs are the result of meticulous planning and a deep understanding of the historical context. Let us embark on a journey through the design elements, inspirations, and visual themes that define the aesthetic landscape of this epic sequel.

The Grandeur of Rome

The heart of "Gladiator 2" lies in the recreation of Rome, the eternal city, pulsating with life, power, and intrigue. The set design aims to capture the city's dual nature: its architectural splendor and its darker, more chaotic underbelly. The Colosseum, a symbol of Rome's might and decadence, stands at the center of this world. Reconstructed with both practical sets and CGI, the Colosseum's towering arches and blood-stained sands are designed to evoke awe and horror, reflecting the glory and brutality of the gladiatorial games.

Inspiration for the Colosseum's design comes from historical records, ancient frescoes, and the remains of the structure itself. The attention to detail is astounding: from the worn stone steps to the intricate carvings on the columns, every element is crafted to transport viewers back in time. The arena's sand, stained with the blood of countless battles, serves as a constant reminder of the cost of Rome's entertainment.

Surrounding the Colosseum, the Forum and the Palatine Hill are brought to life with a blend of grandeur and decay. The Forum, with its bustling markets and towering temples, showcases the architectural brilliance of ancient Rome. Columns and statues, worn by time but still majestic, line the pathways. The Palatine Hill, home to the palaces of the elite, contrasts opulence with the political intrigue that permeates its halls. Richly decorated rooms with mosaics and frescoes tell stories of power and betrayal, each design choice reflecting the complexity of Roman society.

The Provincial Cities and Military Outposts

"Gladiator 2" also takes viewers beyond Rome, to the far-flung provinces and military outposts of the empire. These settings are designed to contrast with the urban splendor of Rome, showcasing the diversity and vastness of the empire. In the deserts of North Africa, the set design captures the stark beauty and harshness of the landscape. Ancient cities like Leptis Magna are recreated with crumbling walls and sun-baked streets, their faded glory hinting at a time when they were bustling centers of trade and culture.

Military outposts on the empire's frontiers are depicted with rugged realism. Fortresses built of stone and timber, surrounded by palisades and watchtowers, reflect the constant state of vigilance required to defend Rome's borders. The interiors of these outposts are Spartan and functional, with barracks, armories, and training grounds. The set design emphasizes the harsh conditions and the disciplined life of the Roman legions stationed far from the comforts of home.

The Aesthetic of Power and Decay

A recurring theme in the set design of "Gladiator 2" is the interplay between power and decay. Rome, at the height of its power, is also shown to be in a state of moral and political decline. This duality is reflected in the design choices throughout the film. Opulent villas and palaces, with their marble floors and gilded statues, stand in stark contrast to the squalid living conditions of the common people. The grandeur of the elite's residences is juxtaposed with the decaying infrastructure of the city, where poverty and corruption fester.

The visual theme of decay extends to the characters' environments. Sejanus's quarters, for example, are luxurious yet shadowy, filled with symbols of power but also hints of the rot beneath the surface. The use of dark, rich colors and heavy fabrics in his rooms creates an atmosphere of opulence laced with menace. In contrast, Lucius's surroundings are designed to reflect his journey from innocence to leadership. His living spaces, initially simple and unadorned, become increasingly sophisticated and strategic as he navigates the treacherous waters of Roman politics.

The Influence of Mythology and Symbolism

Roman mythology and symbolism play a significant role in the aesthetic choices of "Gladiator 2." The gods and their stories are woven into the fabric of the film, influencing the design of both sets and costumes. Temples and altars dedicated to Jupiter, Mars, and other deities are integral parts of the landscape, serving as constant reminders of the divine forces believed to shape human destiny.

Symbolism is also evident in the design of personal spaces and artifacts. Maximus's legacy, for instance, is subtly referenced through symbols associated with his character. The use of lions, eagles, and other Roman icons in the set design and props evokes his strength and leadership. These symbols are strategically placed to enhance the narrative and deepen the connection between the characters and their environments.

The Use of Light and Shadow

The manipulation of light and shadow is a crucial aspect of the film's aesthetic. Ridley Scott and his team use lighting to create mood, emphasize themes, and highlight character development. The interplay of light and darkness reflects the moral complexities and hidden motives that drive the story.

In scenes set in the Colosseum, the harsh, unfiltered light of the sun creates a stark, almost oppressive atmosphere, emphasizing the brutality of the games. In contrast, the interiors of the Senate and the palaces are lit with a softer, more diffused light, creating an aura of mystery and intrigue. The use of candlelight and torches adds a flickering, uncertain quality to these spaces, mirroring the shifting allegiances and hidden agendas of the political elite.

The Natural World

Nature is another significant element in the set design of "Gladiator 2." The natural world is depicted with a reverence for its beauty and power, serving as a counterpoint to the human-made structures of the empire. The film features sweeping landscapes, from the sun-drenched plains of Spain to the misty forests of the northern provinces.

These natural settings are not just backdrops but integral to the story. The forests, with their towering trees and dappled light, provide a refuge for characters fleeing danger or seeking solitude. The open plains and rugged mountains symbolize freedom and the vast, untamed world beyond Rome's control. The natural elements are designed to evoke a sense of awe and respect, highlighting the contrast between the transient nature of human power and the enduring beauty of the natural world.

The Craftsmanship of Props and Costumes

The attention to detail extends to the props and costumes, each piece crafted to enhance the authenticity and richness of the film's world. Weapons, armor, and everyday objects are designed based on historical research, ensuring they reflect the period accurately. The craftsmanship of these items adds to the film's immersive quality, making the world of "Gladiator 2" tangible and believable.

Costumes play a vital role in character development and storytelling. The attire of the characters is meticulously designed to reflect their status, personality, and evolution. Lucius's costumes, for instance, transition from simple tunics to more elaborate and authoritative garments as his character grows into his role as a leader. Sejanus's clothing, rich and opulent, contrasts with the more austere attire of characters like Marcus, highlighting their differing values and motivations.

The Integration of CGI and Practical Effects

While practical sets and real locations form the foundation of the film's visual aesthetic, CGI is used to enhance and extend the world of "Gladiator 2." The integration of digital effects is seamless, creating expansive cityscapes, massive battle scenes, and detailed reconstructions of ancient architecture. The goal is to use technology to support the storytelling without overshadowing the human drama at the heart of the film.

CGI is particularly crucial in scenes that require grand scale, such as the panoramic views of Rome, the teeming crowds of the Colosseum, and the epic battles that define the era. These digital enhancements are designed to blend with the practical sets, ensuring a cohesive and immersive visual experience.

Conclusion

The set design and aesthetic choices for "Gladiator 2" are a testament to the filmmakers' dedication to authenticity, storytelling, and visual splendor. Each element, from the grandeur of Rome to the rugged beauty of the provinces, is crafted to immerse audiences in the world of ancient Rome. The interplay of power and decay, the influence of mythology, and the meticulous attention to detail create a rich, textured backdrop for the epic narrative.

As audiences step into the world of "Gladiator 2," they are not just spectators but participants in a story that spans empires and epochs. The set design and aesthetic choices ensure that this journey is as visually captivating as it is emotionally resonant, honoring the legacy of the original film while forging a new path in cinematic storytelling.

Behind-the-Scenes Insights

The creation of "Gladiator 2" is a story in itself, filled with trials, triumphs, and the relentless pursuit of cinematic excellence. Behind the scenes, a dedicated team of visionaries, artisans, and technicians worked tirelessly to bring the world of ancient Rome to life once more. From the sweeping deserts of Morocco to the historic streets of Rome, every location and set piece was meticulously crafted to evoke the grandeur and grit of the Roman Empire. Here, we delve into the fascinating behind-the-scenes insights, exploring the challenges faced, the creative processes employed, and the anecdotes that shaped the production of this epic sequel.

The Visionary Return of Ridley Scott

The return of Ridley Scott to the director's chair was both a cause for celebration and a monumental challenge. Scott, whose vision defined the original "Gladiator," brought with him a wealth of experience and a clear vision for the sequel. However, the task of recreating the magic of the original while pushing the boundaries of modern filmmaking required a blend of innovation and fidelity to the source material.

Scott's approach was hands-on and immersive. He insisted on shooting in real locations wherever possible, believing that the authenticity of the settings would enhance the film's realism and emotional impact. This decision led the production team to scout and secure some of the most breathtaking and historically resonant locations around the world.

The Challenges of Filming in Morocco

One of the first challenges the team faced was filming in the deserts of Morocco. The decision to shoot in Ouarzazate, known as the "Gateway to the Desert," came with logistical hurdles. The harsh climate, with its scorching daytime temperatures and frigid nights, tested the endurance of the cast and crew. Sandstorms were a frequent and unpredictable menace, often halting production and requiring quick thinking and adaptability from the team.

To combat these challenges, the production team set up a base camp equipped with all the necessary amenities to ensure the comfort and safety of everyone involved. Specialized equipment was brought in to protect the cameras and sensitive electronics from the pervasive dust and sand. Despite these precautions, there were moments when nature's unpredictability tested the limits of technology and patience. One particularly memorable sandstorm buried a significant portion of the set overnight, leading to an impromptu day off while the crew dug out and rebuilt key sections.

Recreating the Colosseum

The Colosseum is central to the world of "Gladiator," and its recreation for the sequel was a monumental task. While the original film used a combination of partial sets and CGI to depict the ancient arena, advancements in technology allowed for even more detailed and immersive representations in "Gladiator 2."

The set construction began with a detailed study of historical documents and archaeological findings. Architects and historians were consulted to ensure accuracy in the design and structure. A significant portion of the Colosseum was built at Cinecittà Studios in Rome, with detailed attention paid to every stone and archway. The practical set allowed actors to perform in an environment that felt authentic, enhancing their performances and the overall realism of the scenes.

For the wider shots, cutting-edge CGI was employed to expand the arena to its full glory. The digital team used photogrammetry and laser scanning techniques to capture every detail of the set, ensuring a seamless blend between the physical and digital elements. This combination of old-school craftsmanship and modern technology resulted in a Colosseum that felt both real and grand, a fitting stage for the epic battles and drama of the film.

Designing the Roman Forum and Palatine Hill

The recreation of the Roman Forum and Palatine Hill was another significant undertaking. These locations are central to the political and social life of ancient Rome and required a level of detail that captured their historical importance and aesthetic grandeur. The production design team, led by the talented Arthur Max, took on the challenge with a mix of passion and precision.

Inspired by ancient texts, frescoes, and existing ruins, the team designed sets that reflected the bustling life of the Forum and the opulence of the Palatine Hill. The Forum's markets, temples, and public spaces were recreated with vibrant detail, from the colorful awnings of the market stalls to the intricate carvings on the temple facades. The Palatine Hill, with its palatial residences and lush gardens, showcased the wealth and power of Rome's elite.

One of the most challenging aspects was ensuring the sets were historically accurate while still serving the narrative needs of the film. This required a balance between archaeological fidelity and creative interpretation. The team built large sections of the Forum and Palatine Hill at Cinecittà Studios, using a mix of traditional set construction and digital extensions to create a seamless and immersive environment.

The Intricacies of Costume Design

Costume design played a crucial role in bringing the characters of "Gladiator 2" to life. Janty Yates, who won an Academy Award for her work on the original film, returned to oversee the costumes for the sequel. Her designs were not just about clothing the characters but about telling their stories through fabric, color, and texture.

Yates's approach was both meticulous and inspired. She sourced materials that would have been available in ancient Rome, ensuring that every garment felt authentic. The colors and patterns used reflected the social status and personality of each character. For instance, Lucius's costumes evolved from simple, youthful tunics to more elaborate and authoritative attire as his character grew into his leadership role. Sejanus's clothing, rich and opulent, contrasted sharply with the more austere attire of characters like Marcus, highlighting their differing values and motivations.

One particularly interesting anecdote involves the creation of Sejanus's armor. Barry Keoghan, who plays Sejanus, worked closely with Yates to develop a look that was both menacing and regal. The armor was handcrafted with intricate detailing, including symbols and motifs that reflected Sejanus's ambition and cunning. During one fitting, Keoghan's input led to the addition of a hidden dagger sheath, a subtle detail that added depth to his character's deceitful nature.

The Technological Innovations

The production of "Gladiator 2" also saw the use of cutting-edge technology to enhance the visual storytelling. One notable innovation was the use of virtual production techniques, similar to those pioneered in "The Mandalorian." This involved the use of LED screens to create realistic backgrounds in real-time, allowing actors to perform in immersive environments without the need for extensive green screen work.

This technology was particularly useful for scenes set in locations that were either too dangerous or logistically challenging to film in. The virtual production allowed for stunning visual effects that felt grounded and realistic, with dynamic lighting and interactive backgrounds that responded to the actors' movements.

The Collaborative Spirit

The production of "Gladiator 2" was a testament to the collaborative spirit of filmmaking. Ridley Scott's leadership and vision brought together a diverse and talented team, each member contributing their expertise to create a cohesive and compelling world. The camaraderie and shared passion were palpable on set, with cast and crew often working long hours to achieve the desired results.

One heartwarming story involves the cast and crew's efforts to support each other during the intense filming schedule. During the Moroccan shoot, where conditions were particularly harsh, a tradition of nightly gatherings around a campfire emerged. These gatherings became a space for relaxation, storytelling, and bonding, helping to foster a sense of community and mutual support. Russell Crowe, who made a special visit to the set, shared anecdotes from the original film, inspiring the new cast with tales of perseverance and dedication.

The Legacy of Maximus

Maximus's legacy was a guiding force throughout the production. The character's impact on the original film and his enduring influence on the sequel were honored in various ways. Russell Crowe's involvement, even if not as an active character, was a significant emotional anchor for the production team. His presence during key moments of the shoot, offering advice and encouragement, helped bridge the gap between the two films.

The production design team also incorporated subtle nods to Maximus in the sets and props. Items associated with him, such as his iconic armor and the figures of his family, were strategically placed to evoke his spirit. These touches were not just for the audience but also served as a source of inspiration for the cast and crew, reminding them of the legacy they were building upon.

Conclusion

The behind-the-scenes story of "Gladiator 2" is one of dedication, innovation, and a deep respect for the source material. The challenges faced and the creative solutions employed speak to the passion and commitment of everyone involved. From the deserts of Morocco to the historic streets of Rome, the production was a journey through time and imagination, bringing to life a world that is both ancient and timeless.

As audiences prepare to return to the Colosseum and the political intrigues of ancient Rome, they can appreciate the immense effort and artistry that went into creating "Gladiator 2." The film is a testament to the power of collaboration and the enduring appeal of epic storytelling, ensuring that the legacy of Maximus Decimus Meridius continues to inspire and captivate.

Special Effects and Cinematography
Advances in Technology Since 2000

The original "Gladiator," released in 2000, was a cinematic marvel, blending practical effects and early CGI to create a visceral and immersive experience. The Colosseum was brought to life with a combination of physical sets and digital extensions, and the battle scenes were choreographed with a raw intensity that still resonates today. Since then, technological advancements have revolutionized the field of special effects and cinematography, offering filmmakers new tools to enhance their storytelling. "Gladiator 2" leverages these innovations to push the boundaries of visual storytelling, creating a world that is even more vivid, detailed, and dynamic.

The Evolution of CGI

Computer-generated imagery (CGI) has undergone a remarkable transformation over the past two decades. In 2000, CGI was still in its relative infancy, with films like "Jurassic Park" and "The Matrix" showcasing its potential but also its limitations. The original "Gladiator" used CGI to extend sets and create crowds in the Colosseum, but the technology was not yet capable of achieving the seamless integration seen in today's films.

For "Gladiator 2," advancements in CGI allow for far more intricate and realistic digital environments. Modern CGI can create photorealistic textures, dynamic lighting, and complex simulations that were unimaginable two decades ago. The sequel employs these technologies to enhance the scale and detail of ancient Rome, from the bustling streets of the Forum to the grandeur of the Colosseum.

One of the key technological advancements is the use of photogrammetry and 3D scanning. These techniques involve capturing high-resolution photographs and scans of real-world objects and environments, which are then used to create highly detailed digital models. For "Gladiator 2," the production team scanned historical sites, artifacts, and even entire landscapes to ensure that the digital recreations were as accurate and immersive as possible.

Real-Time Rendering and Virtual Production

Real-time rendering is another significant advancement that has transformed the filmmaking process. In the past, rendering high-quality CGI scenes could take hours or even days, requiring extensive post-production work. Today, advancements in hardware and software allow for real-time rendering, where CGI elements can be generated instantly and integrated seamlessly into live-action footage.

Virtual production, popularized by series like "The Mandalorian," utilizes LED screens to create immersive environments in real-time. This technology allows actors to perform in front of realistic backgrounds that respond dynamically to camera movements and lighting changes. For "Gladiator 2," virtual production was used to create expansive landscapes and intricate interiors, providing a more immersive experience for the actors and reducing the reliance on green screens.

The use of virtual production also enhances the collaborative process. Directors, cinematographers, and visual effects artists can work together on set, adjusting elements in real-time to achieve the desired look and feel. This level of integration streamlines the production process and allows for greater creative flexibility.

Advances in Motion Capture and Performance Capture

Motion capture technology has come a long way since 2000, evolving from basic tracking systems to sophisticated performance capture that can record the subtlest of facial expressions and body movements. This technology has been crucial in bringing digital characters to life with unprecedented realism and emotional depth.

For "Gladiator 2," performance capture was used to enhance

the portrayal of key characters, particularly in action sequences and scenes requiring complex interactions with CGI elements. Actors wore suits equipped with sensors that tracked their movements and expressions, which were then mapped onto digital models. This technology ensures that the digital performances are grounded in real human emotion and physicality, creating a seamless blend of live-action and CGI.

High-Resolution and High-Dynamic-Range (HDR) Cinematography

The advancements in camera technology have also played a significant role in shaping the visual aesthetic of "Gladiator 2." High-resolution cameras, capable of capturing images in 4K and even 8K, provide an unprecedented level of detail and clarity. This allows filmmakers to create richly textured visuals that draw the audience into the world of the film.

High-dynamic-range (HDR) cinematography further enhances the visual experience by capturing a wider range of light and color. HDR enables filmmakers to create scenes with greater contrast, more vibrant colors, and deeper shadows, adding a level of visual depth that enhances the storytelling. For "Gladiator 2," HDR cinematography was used to capture the stark beauty of the desert landscapes, the intricate details of Roman architecture, and the dramatic lighting of the Colosseum.

Drone Cinematography and Aerial Photography

The use of drones in filmmaking has revolutionized the way aerial shots are captured. Drones provide filmmakers with the ability to achieve dynamic and fluid camera movements that were once only possible with expensive and cumbersome equipment like cranes and helicopters. For "Gladiator 2," drone cinematography was employed to capture sweeping aerial shots of the Colosseum, the bustling streets of Rome, and the vast deserts of North Africa.

These aerial perspectives not only enhance the epic scale of the film but also provide a sense of geographical context and grandeur. The fluidity and flexibility of drone cameras allow for more creative shot compositions, adding a dynamic layer to the visual storytelling.

Practical Effects and Stunt Coordination

While digital effects have made significant strides, practical effects and stunts remain a cornerstone of action filmmaking. "Gladiator 2" combines the best of both worlds, using practical effects to ground the action in reality and CGI to enhance and extend those effects.

The stunt coordination in "Gladiator 2" is a testament to the dedication and skill of the performers and choreographers. Advances in safety equipment and stunt techniques have allowed for more ambitious and complex action sequences. Fight scenes are meticulously choreographed to ensure they are both thrilling and realistic, with actors and stunt performers undergoing rigorous training to perfect their movements.

One of the key innovations in stunt work is the use of previsualization (previs). This technique involves creating detailed digital mockups of action sequences before they are filmed. Previs allows directors and stunt coordinators to plan and visualize the choreography, camera angles, and special effects in advance, ensuring that the final product is both safe and spectacular.

The Soundscape of Ancient Rome

Advancements in sound design and audio technology have also played a crucial role in enhancing the immersive experience of "Gladiator 2." The film's soundscape is meticulously crafted to bring the world of ancient Rome to life, from the bustling markets and roaring crowds of the Colosseum to the quiet whispers of political intrigue.

Dolby Atmos, a cutting-edge sound technology, was used to create a multidimensional audio experience. Unlike traditional surround sound, Dolby Atmos allows for sound to move freely around the theater, creating a more immersive and dynamic auditory environment. This technology enhances the realism of the film, making the audience feel as if they are in the midst of the action.

The film's score, composed by Hans Zimmer and his team, incorporates both traditional orchestral elements and modern soundscapes. The use of ancient instruments, such as the lyre and aulos, blended with contemporary electronic sounds, creates a musical tapestry that reflects the film's themes of legacy and innovation.

The Integration of AI and Machine Learning

Artificial intelligence (AI) and machine learning have also found their way into the filmmaking process. These technologies are used to streamline various aspects of production, from visual effects to editing and color grading.

For "Gladiator 2," AI algorithms were employed to enhance the realism of CGI elements, particularly in the creation of large crowds and complex battle scenes. Machine learning was used to analyze historical data and visual references, helping the production team to achieve a high level of accuracy and authenticity in the set design and costumes.

AI-driven tools also assisted in the post-production process, automating tasks such as rotoscoping, tracking, and compositing. These tools allowed the visual effects team to focus on the creative aspects of their work, ensuring that the final product was both visually stunning and cohesive.

Conclusion

The advances in technology since the release of the original "Gladiator" have transformed the landscape of filmmaking, providing directors, cinematographers, and visual effects artists with an array of new tools to enhance their storytelling. "Gladiator 2" leverages these innovations to create a world that is more immersive, detailed, and dynamic than ever before.

From the seamless integration of CGI and practical effects to the use of real-time rendering and virtual production, the sequel pushes the boundaries of what is possible in cinema. The advancements in motion capture, high-resolution cinematography, and sound design further elevate the film, ensuring that it captures the grandeur and complexity of ancient Rome.

As audiences prepare to return to the Colosseum and witness the epic battles and political intrigues of "Gladiator 2," they can appreciate the technological marvels that have brought this world to life. The film is a testament to the power of innovation and the enduring appeal of epic storytelling, promising to captivate and inspire a new generation of viewers.

Key Visual Elements and Techniques

In "Gladiator 2," the visual storytelling takes center stage, employing a blend of cutting-edge techniques and timeless cinematic artistry to bring the ancient world to life. This film, under Ridley Scott's visionary direction, embraces both the technological advancements of modern filmmaking and the traditional craftsmanship of practical effects. Here, we delve into the key visual elements and techniques that define the aesthetic and narrative power of this epic sequel.

The Cinematic Palette: Color and Light

The visual style of "Gladiator 2" is defined by its rich and dynamic use of color and light. The film's palette is meticulously crafted to reflect the themes and emotional tones of the narrative. Warm, earthy tones dominate the scenes set in the Colosseum and the bustling markets of Rome, evoking the heat and intensity of the gladiatorial combat and the vibrant life of the city. These colors are contrasted with cooler, desaturated hues in the scenes depicting the political machinations and the internal struggles of the characters, highlighting the cold and calculating nature of power.

Lighting plays a crucial role in creating mood and atmosphere. Natural light is used extensively to capture the grandeur of the Roman landscape and the realism of the historical setting. The interplay of light and shadow is employed to enhance the dramatic tension, with chiaroscuro techniques emphasizing the moral ambiguities and hidden agendas of the characters. The flickering torchlight and the soft glow of oil lamps add a layer of authenticity and texture to the night scenes, creating an intimate and immersive experience.

The Colosseum: Reimagined Grandeur

The Colosseum stands as a central visual element in "Gladiator 2," and its recreation showcases a blend of practical sets and advanced CGI. The filmmakers employed photogrammetry and 3D scanning to capture every detail of the ancient structure, ensuring historical accuracy and visual splendor. The practical set at Cinecittà Studios includes a significant portion of the arena, complete with towering arches, stone steps, and the intricate carvings that adorned the original.

To extend the set and create the full scale of the Colosseum, CGI was used seamlessly. This digital extension includes dynamic crowd simulations, where thousands of spectators are brought to life with remarkable realism. Each figure in the crowd is animated individually, reflecting the diversity and energy of the Roman populace. The use of AI and machine learning enhances these simulations, ensuring fluid and natural movements.

Battle Scenes: Choreography and Realism

The battle scenes in "Gladiator 2" are a testament to the meticulous choreography and innovative techniques employed to capture the raw intensity and chaos of combat. Stunt coordinators worked closely with the actors to develop complex fight sequences that are both visually spectacular and grounded in historical authenticity. These scenes were filmed using a combination of handheld cameras and drones, providing dynamic and immersive perspectives.

One of the key innovations in the battle scenes is the use of motion capture for the digital doubles. Actors performed the choreography wearing motion capture suits, which tracked their movements with precision. These performances were then mapped onto digital models, allowing for seamless transitions between live-action and CGI. This technique not only enhances the realism of the combat but also allows for more elaborate and dangerous stunts that would be difficult to achieve practically.

The Use of Virtual Production

Virtual production technology has revolutionized the filmmaking process for "Gladiator 2." The use of LED screens and real-time rendering allows filmmakers to create immersive environments that can be adjusted dynamically during filming. This technique, popularized by "The Mandalorian," enables actors to perform within a fully realized digital environment, reducing the reliance on green screens and enhancing the authenticity of their performances.

For "Gladiator 2," virtual production was used to create expansive landscapes and intricate interiors. The LED screens displayed high-resolution backgrounds that responded to camera movements, providing realistic lighting and reflections. This technology allowed for greater creative flexibility, enabling the filmmakers to visualize and adjust scenes in real-time.

Drone Cinematography and Aerial Shots

The use of drones for aerial cinematography has added a new dimension to the visual storytelling of "Gladiator 2." Drones provide the ability to capture sweeping aerial shots with fluid motion and precision, offering perspectives that were previously difficult to achieve. These aerial views are used to highlight the grandeur of the Colosseum, the vastness of the Roman Empire, and the strategic movements of armies in battle.

The drones are equipped with high-resolution cameras capable of capturing detailed images even in challenging conditions. This technology allows for dynamic shots that follow characters through complex environments, enhancing the sense of scale and movement. The integration of drone footage with ground-based cinematography creates a cohesive and immersive visual experience.

Practical Effects and Set Design

While CGI and digital effects play a significant role, practical effects and set design remain crucial to the authenticity of "Gladiator 2." The production design team, led by Arthur Max, meticulously crafted sets that reflect the architectural and cultural richness of ancient Rome. These sets include detailed recreations of the Forum, the Palatine Hill, and various Roman villas and marketplaces.

The use of practical effects extends to the props and costumes, each piece designed to reflect the period accurately. Weapons, armor, and everyday objects are crafted with historical precision, adding to the film's immersive quality. The practical effects team also created realistic environmental effects, such as dust, smoke, and fire, to enhance the physicality of the scenes.

High-Dynamic-Range (HDR) Cinematography

High-dynamic-range (HDR) cinematography is employed extensively in "Gladiator 2" to capture a wider range of light and color. HDR technology allows for greater contrast and more vibrant colors, enhancing the visual impact of the film. This technique is particularly effective in outdoor scenes, where the play of sunlight and shadow can be rendered with striking realism.

The use of HDR extends to night scenes, where the increased dynamic range allows for deeper blacks and more detailed highlights. The flickering light of torches and the glow of the moon are captured with a richness that adds to the atmospheric depth of the film. HDR also enhances the textures and details of the costumes and sets, making every element of the visual composition more vivid and engaging.

The Soundscape: Immersive Audio Design

The auditory experience of "Gladiator 2" is as meticulously crafted as its visual elements. The sound design incorporates Dolby Atmos technology to create a multidimensional audio environment. This technology allows sound to move freely around the theater, creating an immersive and dynamic auditory experience.

The soundscape of the film includes a blend of diegetic and non-diegetic elements. The roar of the Colosseum crowds, the clash of swords, and the ambient sounds of the Roman streets are combined with Hans Zimmer's evocative score. The use of ancient instruments, such as the lyre and aulos, blended with modern electronic sounds, creates a musical tapestry that enhances the emotional and narrative depth of the film.

Motion Capture and Performance Capture

Motion capture and performance capture technology have been pivotal in bringing the characters of "Gladiator 2" to life with unprecedented realism. This technology allows for the detailed capture of facial expressions and body movements, ensuring that digital characters exhibit the same emotional depth and physical nuance as their live-action counterparts.

Actors performed their scenes wearing motion capture suits equipped with sensors that tracked their movements. These performances were then translated into digital models, allowing for seamless integration with CGI environments. The use of performance capture ensures that the digital representations retain the integrity and subtleties of the actors' performances, creating a cohesive and believable portrayal.

The Integration of AI and Machine Learning

Artificial intelligence (AI) and machine learning are utilized in various aspects of the production process. These technologies assist in enhancing the realism of CGI elements, automating complex tasks, and improving efficiency in post-production.

AI algorithms are used to generate realistic crowd simulations, ensuring fluid and natural movements. Machine learning models analyze historical data and visual references to help the production team achieve high levels of accuracy in set design, costumes, and props. In post-production, AI-driven tools streamline tasks such as rotoscoping, tracking, and compositing, allowing the visual effects team to focus on the creative aspects of their work.

Conclusion

The visual elements and techniques used in "Gladiator 2" represent a harmonious blend of cutting-edge technology and traditional craftsmanship. From the dynamic use of color and light to the seamless integration of CGI and practical effects, every aspect of the film's visual design is meticulously crafted to create an immersive and compelling experience.

Advancements in cinematography, such as HDR and drone technology, enhance the visual storytelling, providing new perspectives and greater detail. Virtual production and real-time rendering revolutionize the filmmaking process, allowing for greater creative flexibility and collaboration. The use of motion capture and AI-driven tools ensures that the digital elements retain the emotional depth and authenticity of the live-action performances.

As audiences prepare to return to the world of ancient Rome, they can look forward to a visual feast that pushes the boundaries of modern filmmaking while honoring the legacy of the original "Gladiator." The film promises to captivate and inspire with its stunning visuals, intricate designs, and innovative techniques, making "Gladiator 2" a landmark achievement in cinematic storytelling.

Collaboration with VFX Studios

In the realm of modern filmmaking, the collaboration between directors and visual effects (VFX) studios is a dance of creativity and technology, a partnership that transforms visions into reality. For "Gladiator 2," the journey back to ancient Rome required the expertise of some of the industry's leading VFX studios. These collaborations were instrumental in bringing the grandeur and brutality of the Roman Empire to life, pushing the boundaries of what is visually possible. Here, we explore the key studios involved, their contributions, and the visual effects achieved, highlighting the intricate web of artistry and innovation that defines the film's visual splendor.

Industrial Light & Magic (ILM)

As pioneers in the field of visual effects, Industrial Light & Magic (ILM) played a crucial role in the creation of "Gladiator 2." Known for their work on iconic films like "Star Wars" and "Jurassic Park," ILM brought their extensive experience and cutting-edge technology to the project. Their primary contributions centered around the reconstruction of the Colosseum and the grand vistas of ancient Rome.

ILM used a combination of photogrammetry and advanced 3D modeling to create a digital Colosseum that is both historically accurate and visually stunning. By scanning existing ruins and historical artifacts, they were able to build a highly detailed model that served as the foundation for many of the film's epic scenes. The digital Colosseum allowed for seamless integration with practical sets, providing a realistic backdrop for the gladiatorial combat and crowd scenes.

The studio also utilized their proprietary real-time rendering technology, enabling the filmmakers to visualize and adjust CGI elements during filming. This innovation ensured that the digital environments matched the lighting and perspective of the live-action footage, creating a cohesive and immersive visual experience.

Weta Digital

Weta Digital, the New Zealand-based VFX studio renowned for their work on "The Lord of the Rings" and "Avatar," contributed significantly to the complex battle scenes and character animations in "Gladiator 2." Their expertise in motion capture and digital doubles was crucial in achieving the film's intense and realistic combat sequences.

The collaboration with Weta Digital involved the use of advanced motion capture technology to record the performances of the actors and stunt performers. These performances were then translated into highly detailed digital models, allowing for intricate and dynamic fight choreography that would be challenging to film practically. Weta's motion capture facilities, equipped with the latest technology, captured every nuance of the actors' movements, ensuring that the digital doubles exhibited the same physicality and emotion as their real-life counterparts.

In addition to the battle scenes, Weta Digital was responsible for creating the vast armies and intricate crowd simulations. Using their proprietary MASSIVE software, they generated thousands of individual characters, each with their own unique behaviors and interactions. This technology brought the chaotic and vibrant world of ancient Rome to life, filling the Colosseum and the battlefields with realistic and dynamic crowds.

Framestore

Framestore, a VFX studio with a legacy of award-winning work on films like "Gravity" and "Blade Runner 2049," focused on the environmental effects and the seamless integration of CGI with practical elements. Their contributions included the creation of realistic natural environments and the enhancement of practical effects with digital artistry.

One of Framestore's major tasks was the depiction of the North African deserts and the Roman countryside. By combining high-resolution aerial photography with digital terrain modeling, they crafted expansive landscapes that provided a stunning backdrop for the film's epic journey sequences. These digital environments were meticulously detailed, capturing the texture of the sand, the play of light and shadow, and the subtle variations in the landscape.

Framestore also enhanced the practical effects with digital augmentation. For instance, in scenes involving fire and smoke, they used fluid dynamics simulations to create realistic and dynamic effects that blended seamlessly with the live-action footage. This approach allowed the filmmakers to achieve a high level of visual fidelity while maintaining the safety and control of practical effects.

MPC (Moving Picture Company)

The Moving Picture Company (MPC), known for their work on "The Jungle Book" and "The Lion King," brought their expertise in creature effects and digital makeup to "Gladiator 2." Their role was pivotal in creating the film's more fantastical elements and in enhancing the physical performances of the actors.

MPC's work included the creation of digital creatures and animals that populated the world of "Gladiator 2." Using a combination of motion capture and keyframe animation, they brought these creatures to life with a high degree of realism. Their attention to detail ensured that the creatures' movements and behaviors were natural and believable, adding depth and immersion to the film's environment.

Additionally, MPC was responsible for digital makeup and de-aging effects, allowing the filmmakers to portray characters at different ages and with various physical alterations. This technology was used to enhance the performances of the actors, ensuring continuity and realism throughout the film.

The Art of Collaboration

The collaboration between these VFX studios and the production team of "Gladiator 2" was characterized by a shared vision and a commitment to excellence. Regular meetings and workshops were held to ensure that the creative and technical teams were aligned, with each studio contributing their unique expertise to the project. This collaborative approach allowed for the seamless integration of various visual elements, creating a cohesive and visually stunning final product.

One of the key aspects of this collaboration was the use of previsualization (previs) to plan and refine the visual effects sequences. Previs involved creating detailed digital mockups of the scenes, allowing the filmmakers to experiment with different camera angles, lighting setups, and visual effects before the actual filming began. This process helped to streamline the production, reduce costs, and ensure that the final scenes matched the director's vision.

Challenges and Innovations

The production of "Gladiator 2" was not without its challenges. The integration of practical and digital effects required precise coordination and attention to detail. One of the significant challenges was ensuring that the digital environments matched the physical sets in terms of lighting, texture, and perspective. This was achieved through the use of advanced lighting simulation and real-time rendering, allowing the VFX teams to match the digital elements to the live-action footage with high accuracy.

Another challenge was the creation of realistic and dynamic crowd simulations. The VFX teams employed AI-driven technologies to generate thousands of individual characters, each with their own unique behaviors and interactions. This technology ensured that the crowds in the Colosseum and the battlefields felt alive and dynamic, enhancing the overall realism of the film.

The Impact of Technology

The technological advancements in visual effects and cinematography have significantly impacted the production of "Gladiator 2." The collaboration with leading VFX studios has enabled the filmmakers to push the boundaries of visual storytelling, creating a world that is both historically accurate and visually stunning. The use of real-time rendering, motion capture, and AI-driven crowd simulations has enhanced the realism and immersion of the film, bringing the ancient world to life in ways that were previously unimaginable.

Conclusion

The collaboration with VFX studios for "Gladiator 2" is a testament to the power of teamwork and innovation in modern filmmaking. The contributions of ILM, Weta Digital, Framestore, and MPC have been instrumental in creating the film's breathtaking visual effects, blending practical craftsmanship with cutting-edge technology. This partnership has not only enhanced the visual storytelling but also ensured that the legacy of the original "Gladiator" is honored and expanded in new and exciting ways. As audiences prepare to return to the world of ancient Rome, they can look forward to a visual feast that pushes the boundaries of cinematic artistry.

Music and Score

Composer Overview

In the symphonic landscape of "Gladiator 2," the melodies and harmonies that guide our emotions and elevate the narrative are crafted by none other than the legendary Hans Zimmer. Renowned for his ability to blend traditional orchestration with innovative electronic elements, Zimmer's music has become synonymous with cinematic grandeur and emotional depth. His return to score the sequel to the iconic "Gladiator" promises to weave a tapestry of sound that is both familiar and refreshingly new, an auditory journey that will echo through the ages.

The Early Years

Hans Zimmer was born on September 12, 1957, in Frankfurt, Germany. From a young age, Zimmer showed an affinity for music, a passion that was nurtured in the contrasting worlds of classical and modern sounds. His early influences included the works of classical composers such as Beethoven and Mozart, as well as the emerging electronic music scene. This eclectic mix of influences would later define Zimmer's unique style, characterized by a seamless fusion of orchestral and electronic elements.

Zimmer's career began in earnest when he moved to London and joined the band The Buggles, where he played keyboards on their hit single "Video Killed the Radio Star." This foray into the world of pop music was a stepping stone to his true calling: composing for film. His transition to film scoring was facilitated by his collaboration with composer Stanley Myers, with whom he co-founded the Lillie Yard recording studio. Together, they worked on various film scores, blending traditional orchestration with modern synthesizers.

Breakthrough and Style Evolution

Zimmer's big break came with the 1988 film "Rain Man," for which he received his first Academy Award nomination.

The score showcased Zimmer's talent for creating emotionally resonant music that could subtly underscore the narrative without overwhelming it. This ability to balance emotion and restraint became a hallmark of his style, earning him a place among the top composers in Hollywood.

The 1990s saw Zimmer's star rise further with a string of successful scores. His work on "The Lion King" (1994) earned him an Academy Award, a Golden Globe, and two Grammy Awards. The score, featuring African rhythms and choral arrangements, demonstrated Zimmer's versatility and willingness to explore new musical landscapes. This period also saw the creation of iconic scores for films such as "Crimson Tide" (1995), "The Rock" (1996), and "Gladiator" (2000).

The Original "Gladiator" Score

The score for Ridley Scott's "Gladiator" is arguably one of Zimmer's most celebrated works. Collaborating with vocalist Lisa Gerrard, Zimmer crafted a soundtrack that was both epic and intimate, capturing the grandeur of ancient Rome and the personal tragedy of Maximus Decimus Meridius. The music's blend of sweeping orchestral themes and haunting vocal performances created a timeless soundscape that resonated deeply with audiences and critics alike.

The success of the "Gladiator" score cemented Zimmer's reputation as a master of cinematic music. The soundtrack album sold millions of copies worldwide and received numerous awards, including a Golden Globe for Best Original Score. The themes from "Gladiator," such as "Now We Are Free" and "The Battle," have since become iconic, often used in trailers, commercials, and even sporting events.

Continued Success and Innovation

Following "Gladiator," Zimmer continued to push the boundaries of film scoring. His work on Christopher Nolan's "The Dark Knight Trilogy" (2005-2012) redefined the sound of superhero films, with its dark, brooding motifs and innovative use of electronic textures. The "Inception" (2010) score, with its iconic "BRAAAM" sound, further showcased Zimmer's ability to create unforgettable auditory experiences.

Zimmer's collaboration with director Denis Villeneuve on "Dune" (2021) marked another milestone in his career. The score, which blended traditional orchestration with experimental sounds and instruments, earned Zimmer his second Academy Award. It was a testament to his relentless pursuit of new musical frontiers and his ability to adapt his style to fit the unique vision of each film.

Returning to the Arena: "Gladiator 2"

The announcement that Hans Zimmer would return to score "Gladiator 2" was met with widespread excitement. Fans of the original film eagerly anticipated how Zimmer would revisit and expand upon the themes that had made the first soundtrack so memorable. For Zimmer, the project presented an opportunity to delve deeper into the musical motifs he had created two decades earlier, while also exploring new sonic territories.

In "Gladiator 2," Zimmer faces the challenge of honoring the legacy of the original score while crafting a new auditory journey that reflects the sequel's narrative evolution. He aims to weave together the familiar themes of heroism, sacrifice, and revenge with new musical elements that capture the expanded scope and complexity of the story.

Zimmer's approach to the score is expected to incorporate a blend of traditional orchestration and modern electronic elements, a signature of his style. He has hinted at the inclusion of new vocal performances, perhaps collaborating once again with Lisa Gerrard or other vocalists to create haunting, ethereal melodies that evoke the spirit of ancient Rome.

The Soundscape of "Gladiator 2"

The music of "Gladiator 2" is poised to be a dynamic and multifaceted soundscape. Zimmer's use of leitmotifs—recurring musical themes associated with specific characters or ideas—will likely play a significant role in the score. These leitmotifs will help to create a sense of continuity and cohesion, linking the sequel to the original film while also introducing new themes that reflect the evolving narrative.

Zimmer's orchestration will likely draw on a rich palette of instruments, blending traditional Roman and Mediterranean sounds with modern orchestral techniques. Expect the use of ancient instruments such as the lyre, aulos, and Roman trumpet, woven seamlessly with the lush strings and powerful brass of a full orchestra. Electronic elements, including synthesized textures and rhythmic patterns, will add a contemporary edge, creating a sound that is both timeless and cutting-edge.

A Composer's Legacy

Hans Zimmer's return to the world of "Gladiator" is not just a continuation of a musical journey, but a celebration of a legacy that has left an indelible mark on cinematic history. His ability to create music that transcends the screen, resonating with audiences on a deep emotional level, is a testament to his genius. Zimmer's scores are more than just soundtracks; they are integral components of the films they accompany, enhancing the storytelling and elevating the visual experience.

As "Gladiator 2" prepares to take audiences back to the sands of the Colosseum, Zimmer's music will once again serve as the heartbeat of the film, guiding us through the epic battles, intimate moments, and sweeping vistas of ancient Rome. His mastery of melody, harmony, and rhythm will ensure that the soundtrack of "Gladiator 2" is as iconic and unforgettable as that of its predecessor.

In a career spanning over four decades, Hans Zimmer has continually redefined what is possible in film music. His work on "Gladiator 2" is poised to be another milestone in his illustrious career, a testament to his enduring talent and his ability to capture the essence of a story through the power of music. As the echoes of the Colosseum roar to life once more, Zimmer's score will remind us why he is one of the greatest composers of our time, a true maestro of the cinematic soundscape.

Musical Themes and Influence

In "Gladiator 2," the soundtrack crafted by Hans Zimmer promises to be a powerful extension of the musical landscape established in the original film, enriched with new themes and influences that reflect the evolving narrative. Zimmer's approach to scoring the sequel intertwines the haunting melodies of ancient Rome with modern musical sensibilities, creating a soundscape that is both epic and intimate. The musical themes and motifs are designed to evoke the grandeur of the Roman Empire, the intensity of gladiatorial combat, and the deep emotional currents that drive the story.

The Hero's Legacy: Lucius's Theme

At the heart of "Gladiator 2" is the character of Lucius Verus, whose journey from innocence to leadership is a central narrative thread. Zimmer's musical theme for Lucius reflects this transformation, capturing the character's inner conflict and burgeoning strength. The theme is built around a simple, noble melody played on the lyre, an instrument deeply rooted in ancient Roman culture. This motif evolves throughout the film, mirroring Lucius's development as he grapples with the legacy of Maximus and his own destiny.

The lyre's delicate notes are often accompanied by a full orchestra, with strings and brass swelling to underscore moments of triumph and introspection. As Lucius faces the challenges of leadership, the theme incorporates more complex harmonies and darker tones, reflecting the weight of responsibility and the sacrifices required to achieve his goals. The evolution of Lucius's theme serves as a musical narrative, guiding the audience through his emotional and psychological journey.

The Shadow of Ambition: Sejanus's Theme

Sejanus, the ambitious antagonist of "Gladiator 2," is portrayed through a motif that exudes cunning and menace. Zimmer uses dissonant harmonies and sharp, staccato rhythms to create a sense of tension and unpredictability. The primary instrument for Sejanus's theme is the kithara, another ancient string instrument, but it is played with an aggressive, almost percussive style that underscores his ruthless nature.

This theme often employs minor keys and irregular time signatures, enhancing the sense of unease and danger associated with Sejanus. Electronic elements are subtly woven into the motif, creating a modern edge that reflects his strategic mind and relentless pursuit of power. As Sejanus's machinations unfold, his theme becomes more prominent and layered, illustrating his growing influence and the peril he poses to Lucius and Rome.

Echoes of the Past: Maximus's Legacy

The legacy of Maximus Decimus Meridius looms large over "Gladiator 2," and Zimmer pays homage to the original film with recurring musical references to Maximus's theme. These echoes are woven into the new score, creating a sense of continuity and honoring the heroism that defined Maximus's character. The motif is introduced through a haunting vocal line, often performed by a solo female voice, evoking the memory of Lisa Gerrard's iconic contributions to the first film.

Maximus's theme is used sparingly but powerfully, surfacing at pivotal moments to remind characters and audiences alike of his enduring influence. The orchestration of these passages is rich and emotional, blending strings, horns, and choral elements to create a sound that is both reverent and inspirational. This musical continuity helps to bridge the gap between the original "Gladiator" and its sequel, ensuring that Maximus's spirit remains a guiding force.

The Colosseum's Roar: Battle Themes

The gladiatorial combats in "Gladiator 2" are accompanied by some of the most dynamic and intense music Zimmer has composed. The battle themes are characterized by driving rhythms, powerful brass sections, and intricate percussion, capturing the ferocity and chaos of the arena. These pieces often begin with a steady, relentless beat, building in intensity as the combat progresses.

Zimmer employs a variety of percussion instruments, including traditional Roman drums and modern cinematic impacts, to create a visceral auditory experience. The use of syncopation and complex time signatures adds to the sense of unpredictability and danger. Brass fanfares and aggressive string ostinatos underscore the heroism and desperation of the gladiators, providing a musical counterpart to the visual spectacle of the battles.

In quieter moments within the arena, a solo instrument such as a duduk or flute may emerge, offering a brief respite and highlighting the personal stakes for the characters involved. These interludes serve to humanize the combatants, reminding the audience of their individual stories and struggles.

The Political Intrigue: Themes of Deception and Strategy

The political landscape of ancient Rome is fraught with intrigue and betrayal, and Zimmer's score reflects this through a series of motifs that underscore the themes of deception and strategy. These themes are often marked by subtle, insidious melodies played on woodwinds and strings, creating an atmosphere of suspicion and tension.

The motif for political intrigue frequently employs counterpoint and layered textures, mirroring the complex interplay of alliances and rivalries within the Senate and the imperial court. Pizzicato strings and muted brass add a sense of stealth and cunning, while dissonant harmonies reflect the moral ambiguities and shifting loyalties that characterize the political arena.

Electronic elements are also integrated into these themes, providing a modern sonic layer that complements the historical setting. This fusion of old and new highlights the timeless nature of power struggles and the universal themes of ambition and manipulation.

The Heart of Rome: Cultural and Regional Influences

Zimmer's score for "Gladiator 2" is deeply informed by the rich cultural and musical heritage of ancient Rome and its provinces. The soundtrack incorporates a variety of traditional instruments and musical styles from across the Roman Empire, creating a diverse and textured auditory landscape.

For scenes set in North Africa, Zimmer employs instruments such as the oud and the darbouka, blending Middle Eastern melodies and rhythms with the orchestral score. These elements provide a sense of place and authenticity, immersing the audience in the diverse cultural tapestry of the Roman world.

Similarly, for sequences set in the Mediterranean regions, instruments like the bouzouki and the Greek lyra are featured, adding regional color and enhancing the historical atmosphere. This approach not only enriches the musical palette but also underscores the vast reach and influence of the Roman Empire.

The Emotional Core: Themes of Love and Loss

At the heart of "Gladiator 2" are the themes of love and loss, explored through poignant and deeply emotional music. Zimmer crafts these themes with delicate, lyrical melodies that capture the intimate moments of the film. The love theme, associated with Lucius and his relationships, is characterized by tender strings and piano, creating a sense of warmth and vulnerability.

The motif for loss, which recurs throughout the film, is often introduced by a solo instrument, such as a cello or a violin, conveying a deep sense of melancholy and reflection. These themes are harmonically rich and emotionally resonant, providing a counterpoint to the more action-oriented music and grounding the film in its human stories.

The interplay between the love and loss motifs creates a dynamic emotional landscape, reflecting the characters' internal struggles and the broader narrative arcs. Zimmer's ability to weave these themes into the fabric of the score ensures that the music remains deeply connected to the story and its characters.

Innovation and Tradition: Zimmer's Signature Blend

Hans Zimmer's work on "Gladiator 2" exemplifies his signature blend of innovation and tradition. The score seamlessly integrates traditional orchestration with electronic elements, creating a sound that is both timeless and contemporary. Zimmer's use of advanced recording techniques and modern technology, combined with his deep understanding of historical musical practices, results in a soundtrack that is richly layered and profoundly impactful.

One of the innovative aspects of Zimmer's approach is his use of spatial audio techniques, which create a three-dimensional soundscape. This technology enhances the immersive quality of the music, allowing the audience to experience the score in a more dynamic and enveloping way. By placing instruments and sounds within a spatial context, Zimmer adds depth and dimension to the musical experience, making it an integral part of the film's storytelling.

Conclusion

The musical themes and influences in "Gladiator 2" are a testament to Hans Zimmer's genius and his ability to craft scores that resonate deeply with audiences. Through a combination of traditional orchestration, innovative technology, and a profound understanding of the film's narrative, Zimmer creates a soundtrack that is both epic and intimate, capturing the grandeur of ancient Rome and the personal stories of its characters.

From the heroic motifs of Lucius to the menacing themes of Sejanus, the haunting echoes of Maximus's legacy, and the rich cultural influences that permeate the score, the music of "Gladiator 2" is a dynamic and multifaceted tapestry. It is a journey through sound that mirrors the epic journey of the film, guiding the audience through the highs and lows, the battles and the triumphs, and the deep emotional currents that define the story.

As "Gladiator 2" unfolds on the screen, Zimmer's music will be its heartbeat, a powerful and evocative force that brings the ancient world to life and ensures that the legacy of "Gladiator" continues to inspire and captivate.

Anticipated Soundtrack Highlights

As the echoes of the Colosseum once more reverberate through the corridors of time, the soundtrack of "Gladiator 2" promises to be an auditory journey that will captivate and inspire. Crafted by the legendary Hans Zimmer, the score is anticipated to deliver a rich tapestry of sound, blending the familiar themes of the original film with new, evocative compositions. Here, we delve into the anticipated highlights of this epic soundtrack, exploring key tracks, insights from the composer, and the expected impact on audiences.

1. "Lucius's Ascension"

One of the most anticipated tracks is "Lucius's Ascension," a piece that encapsulates the journey of Lucius Verus as he steps into his role as a leader. The track is expected to open with a delicate motif played on the lyre, symbolizing Lucius's noble lineage and the influence of Maximus. As the piece progresses, it will evolve into a full orchestral arrangement, with swelling strings and powerful brass sections that underscore his growing strength and resolve.

Hans Zimmer has hinted that this track will incorporate both traditional Roman instruments and modern electronic elements, creating a soundscape that is both timeless and contemporary. The crescendo of the piece is likely to be a moment of musical triumph, reflecting Lucius's acceptance of his destiny and his determination to restore honor to Rome.

2. "The Arena"

"The Arena" is anticipated to be one of the most dynamic and intense tracks on the soundtrack, capturing the raw energy and brutal spectacle of the gladiatorial combats. Zimmer's use of driving rhythms, intricate percussion, and aggressive brass will bring the chaos and adrenaline of the arena to life. The track will likely begin with a steady, ominous beat, building tension before erupting into a frenetic orchestral onslaught as the battle ensues.

This piece is expected to showcase Zimmer's mastery of combining orchestral and electronic elements, with layered textures that add depth and complexity to the sound. The inclusion of traditional Roman percussion instruments, such as the timpani and the tuba, will enhance the authenticity and visceral impact of the music. "The Arena" is poised to be a standout track that immerses listeners in the heart-pounding action of the gladiatorial games.

3. "Echoes of Maximus"

A poignant and emotionally charged piece, "Echoes of Maximus" will pay homage to the fallen hero whose legacy looms large over the sequel. This track is expected to feature the haunting vocal lines that characterized the original score, perhaps with Lisa Gerrard returning to lend her ethereal voice once more. The use of solo instruments, such as the cello and the duduk, will add a layer of melancholy and reflection, evoking the memory of Maximus and his enduring influence.

Zimmer has mentioned that this track will be a meditative exploration of loss and remembrance, blending familiar themes from the first film with new, introspective melodies. "Echoes of Maximus" is likely to be a deeply moving piece that resonates with fans of the original "Gladiator," reminding them of the hero's sacrifices and the timeless impact of his story.

4. "Sejanus's Machinations"

"Sejanus's Machinations" is expected to be a track that delves into the darker, more sinister aspects of the narrative. This piece will likely feature dissonant harmonies and sharp, staccato rhythms that create a sense of tension and unease. The primary instrument for this track is anticipated to be the kithara, played in an aggressive and percussive style that underscores Sejanus's ruthless ambition.

Zimmer has suggested that this track will incorporate electronic elements to enhance the sense of modernity and strategic cunning associated with Sejanus. The use of minor keys and irregular time signatures will add to the sense of unpredictability and danger, making "Sejanus's Machinations" a thrilling and foreboding highlight of the soundtrack.

5. "The Heart of Rome"

"The Heart of Rome" is anticipated to be a sweeping, grandiose piece that captures the cultural and architectural splendor of the ancient city. This track will likely feature lush orchestral arrangements, with a prominent role for strings and woodwinds that evoke the vibrancy and complexity of Rome. The inclusion of traditional Roman instruments, such as the lyre and the aulos, will add a layer of historical authenticity and richness to the sound.

Zimmer's use of spatial audio techniques is expected to enhance the immersive quality of this track, creating a three-dimensional auditory experience that transports listeners to the bustling streets and majestic temples of Rome. "The Heart of Rome" will be a celebration of the city's grandeur and a reminder of its enduring legacy.

6. "The Journey"

"The Journey" is expected to be a track that encapsulates the epic scope of the film, following the characters as they traverse the diverse landscapes of the Roman Empire. This piece will likely feature a blend of regional musical influences, incorporating instruments and melodies from North Africa, the Mediterranean, and the northern provinces. The use of the oud, bouzouki, and other traditional instruments will add cultural texture and depth to the composition.

Zimmer has indicated that this track will be a musical odyssey, with shifting dynamics and themes that reflect the changing environments and challenges faced by the characters. "The Journey" is anticipated to be a richly layered piece that captures the vastness and diversity of the Roman world, enhancing the film's sense of adventure and exploration.

7. "Love and Loss"

"Love and Loss" is expected to be one of the most emotionally resonant tracks on the soundtrack, exploring the themes of romance and tragedy that underpin the narrative. This piece will likely feature tender piano melodies and soaring string arrangements, creating a sense of intimacy and vulnerability. The use of solo instruments, such as the violin and the flute, will add a layer of poignancy and depth to the music.

Zimmer's ability to convey deep emotion through his compositions will be on full display in this track, which is expected to be a heart-wrenching exploration of the characters' personal struggles and sacrifices. "Love and Loss" will be a musical highlight that touches the audience's hearts and underscores the human drama at the core of "Gladiator 2."

Conclusion

The anticipated soundtrack highlights for "Gladiator 2" promise to deliver a rich and diverse auditory experience that enhances the film's epic narrative. Hans Zimmer's masterful blend of traditional orchestration, innovative electronic elements, and deep emotional resonance ensures that each track will leave a lasting impression. From the heroic motifs of "Lucius's Ascension" to the intense rhythms of "The Arena," and the poignant reflections of "Echoes of Maximus," the soundtrack will be a powerful force that guides the audience through the grandeur and intimacy of the story.

As fans eagerly await the release of "Gladiator 2," they can look forward to a soundtrack that not only honors the legacy of the original film but also expands upon it with new, evocative compositions. Zimmer's music will be the heartbeat of the film, a dynamic and multifaceted tapestry that brings the ancient world to life and ensures that the legacy of "Gladiator" continues to inspire and captivate.

Marketing and Promotion

Trailer and Teaser Analysis

The anticipation for "Gladiator 2" has been palpable, and the release of its trailers and teasers has only intensified the excitement. Each frame, each cut, each note of the accompanying music has been meticulously crafted to evoke the grandeur and emotional depth of the original while teasing the new epic tale. Let's delve into the trailers and teasers, exploring the key elements, themes, and visual cues that have set the stage for this cinematic return to ancient Rome.

The First Teaser: A Glimpse into the Arena

The initial teaser for "Gladiator 2" offers a tantalizing glimpse into the world of the film. The teaser opens with a sweeping aerial shot of the Colosseum, its massive arches and towering stands rendered in breathtaking detail. The camera swoops down, giving viewers a sense of the scale and grandeur of this iconic structure. Dust rises from the arena floor, the echoes of past battles whispering through the air.

Immediately, the teaser establishes a connection to the original film with the familiar strains of Hans Zimmer's score, reimagined with new layers and textures. This auditory cue sets the tone, creating an emotional bridge between the two films. The teaser then cuts to a close-up of Lucius Verus (Paul Mescal), his face shadowed but resolute, eyes reflecting the weight of his legacy. The camera lingers, allowing the audience to connect with the character's internal struggle.

Quick, dynamic cuts follow, showcasing snippets of gladiatorial combat. The choreography is intense, brutal, and beautifully shot, with each strike and parry captured in exquisite detail. The use of slow motion heightens the drama, emphasizing the raw power and skill of the fighters. The teaser's pacing quickens, interspersing scenes of political intrigue with moments of personal reflection, hinting at the film's multifaceted narrative.

The Main Trailer: Expanding the Narrative

The main trailer expands upon the initial teaser, providing a broader look at the story and characters. It opens with a voiceover, deep and resonant, setting the stage: "Rome stands on the brink, its heart in the hands of a new generation." This line, coupled with visuals of the city in both grandeur and decay, establishes the stakes.

The trailer introduces new characters, each given a moment that hints at their role and personality. Sejanus (Barry Keoghan) is depicted in shadowy council chambers, his eyes calculating and cold. His theme, a discordant blend of strings and electronic pulses, underscores his sinister ambition. Julia (Jodie Comer) is shown navigating the opulent yet dangerous halls of power, her face a mask of determination and subtle fear.

Lucius's journey is a central focus. The trailer shows him training, forging alliances, and grappling with his inherited legacy. A poignant moment is highlighted where Lucius stands before a statue of Maximus, the music swelling to a familiar yet newly orchestrated theme. This visual and auditory callback to the original film underscores the weight of expectation and the drive for justice that propels Lucius.

The trailer's editing is masterful, balancing quiet, character-driven moments with scenes of epic scale. Battle sequences are intercut with political machinations, creating a sense of urgency and impending conflict. The use of color grading is notable; the warm, sun-drenched hues of Rome contrast sharply with the cold, muted tones of the Senate chambers, visually reinforcing the thematic dichotomy of honor versus corruption.

Visual and Thematic Cues

The visual style of "Gladiator 2," as showcased in the trailers, is rich and evocative. The filmmakers have employed a blend of practical effects and CGI to recreate ancient Rome with stunning realism. The Colosseum, a focal point, is depicted with a level of detail that surpasses the original, thanks to advancements in technology. The textures of the stone, the wear and tear of years of combat, and the play of light and shadow all contribute to an immersive experience.

The trailers also highlight the film's thematic depth. The recurring motif of legacy is visually represented through symbols and artifacts—Maximus's armor, the Colosseum itself, and the familial emblems of the characters. The contrast between the ideals of the past and the realities of the present is a central theme, underscored by the visual juxtaposition of Rome's glory and its decay.

Political intrigue is another prominent theme, with the trailers showcasing the labyrinthine corridors of power. The lighting in these scenes is deliberate, with deep shadows and stark contrasts reflecting the murky ethics and hidden agendas of Rome's elite. The use of mirrors and reflective surfaces further symbolizes the duplicity and deception at play.

Music and Sound Design

Hans Zimmer's score, a critical element in the trailers, plays a significant role in setting the tone. The music transitions from the haunting melodies associated with Maximus to new, dynamic themes that reflect the evolving narrative. The blend of traditional orchestral arrangements with electronic elements creates a soundscape that is both familiar and fresh.

Sound design is also crucial, with the trailers employing a mix of diegetic and non-diegetic sounds to enhance the immersive quality. The roar of the Colosseum crowds, the clashing of swords, and the ambient sounds of Rome's streets are interwoven with the score, creating a rich auditory experience. Moments of silence or subdued sound are used effectively to heighten tension and focus attention on the visual storytelling.

Character Dynamics and Plot Hints

The trailers and teasers offer tantalizing glimpses into the character dynamics and plot twists. Lucius's interactions with

Sejanus and Julia are charged with tension, hinting at alliances and conflicts that will drive the story. The visual language —glances, body language, and spatial relationships—suggests complex interpersonal dynamics that will be explored in the film.

The trailers hint at several key plot points without giving away too much. Scenes of clandestine meetings, coded messages, and covert actions suggest a plot thick with intrigue and betrayal. The glimpses of battle scenes indicate that physical combat will be a significant aspect of the film, but the true battleground lies in the halls of power and within the characters' hearts.

Audience Reception and Anticipation

The release of the trailers has generated significant buzz and anticipation. Fans of the original "Gladiator" are eager to see how the sequel will honor its predecessor while forging its own path. The trailers have been praised for their visual fidelity, emotional depth, and the tantalizing glimpses of the narrative.

Critics and fans alike have noted the trailers' ability to balance nostalgia with innovation. The callbacks to the original film, both visual and musical, are appreciated for their subtlety and reverence. Meanwhile, the introduction of new characters and plot elements promises a fresh and engaging story that stands on its own merits.

Conclusion

The trailers and teasers for "Gladiator 2" have masterfully set the stage for an epic cinematic experience. Through a blend of stunning visuals, evocative music, and thematic depth, they have managed to honor the legacy of the original film while promising a new and compelling narrative. The careful balance of character-driven storytelling and grand spectacle ensures that audiences are eagerly anticipating the film's release.

As we await the full return to the Colosseum and the world of ancient Rome, the trailers have done their job brilliantly—

captivating the imagination, stirring the emotions, and leaving us longing for more. In the hands of Ridley Scott and Hans Zimmer, "Gladiator 2" is poised to be a triumphant continuation of a beloved saga, one that will echo through the annals of cinematic history.

Marketing Strategies and Campaigns

The marketing strategies and campaigns for "Gladiator 2" are a carefully orchestrated symphony, designed to build anticipation, captivate audiences, and ensure the film's grand return to the silver screen is nothing short of spectacular. Leveraging a blend of traditional advertising, innovative social media campaigns, and immersive promotional activities, the marketing team has crafted a multi-faceted approach that resonates with both fans of the original and a new generation of moviegoers.

Teaser Campaign: Building Early Buzz

The marketing journey for "Gladiator 2" began with a series of enigmatic teasers. Months before the official trailer dropped, short, cryptic videos and images were released across various platforms. These teasers featured iconic symbols from the original film—Maximus's helmet, the Colosseum's shadowy arches, and the haunting strains of Hans Zimmer's score—each designed to evoke nostalgia and curiosity.

The teasers were strategically timed to coincide with major entertainment events, such as the Super Bowl and Comic-Con. At the Super Bowl, a 30-second spot aired, featuring rapid cuts of battle scenes and the new protagonist, Lucius Verus, set to the pulse-pounding rhythms of Zimmer's music. This brief yet powerful glimpse immediately sparked conversation, with social media platforms lighting up with speculation and excitement.

Trailer Releases: Capturing the Imagination

The release of the full trailer was an event in itself, unveiled simultaneously across multiple platforms including YouTube, Instagram, and Twitter. The trailer premiere was accompanied by a live Q&A session with director Ridley Scott and key cast members, streamed on YouTube and Facebook Live. This interactive element allowed fans to engage directly with the creators, asking questions and receiving insights into the making of the film.

The trailer was also showcased in cinemas, preceding blockbuster movies to maximize its reach. The use of Dolby Atmos sound and IMAX screenings ensured that the audiovisual impact was felt in its full glory, immersing audiences in the world of ancient Rome. The cinematic release of the trailer was timed with a coordinated online campaign, with official posters and character profiles shared on social media, creating a cohesive and immersive promotional push.

Social Media Campaigns: Engaging the Digital Audience

Social media has played a pivotal role in the marketing of "Gladiator 2." The film's official accounts on platforms like Instagram, Twitter, and TikTok have been buzzing with activity, offering fans a steady stream of content to maintain excitement and engagement. These platforms have been used to share behind-the-scenes footage, character spotlights, and thematic insights, each piece crafted to deepen the audience's connection with the film.

Instagram, with its visual focus, has been a hub for exclusive images and short video clips. High-quality stills from the film, character portraits, and scenic shots of Rome and the Colosseum have been regularly posted, accompanied by engaging captions and hashtags. Instagram Stories and Reels have been used to share snippets of cast interviews, set tours, and fan reactions, creating a dynamic and interactive experience.

Twitter has been the platform for real-time updates and fan interaction. The marketing team has orchestrated hashtag campaigns like #ReturnToTheColosseum and #Gladiator2, encouraging fans to share their excitement, theories, and fan art. Regular retweets and replies from the official account have fostered a sense of community and inclusivity, making fans feel like active participants in the film's journey.

TikTok, with its younger demographic and emphasis on short-form video content, has been used to reach a new generation of potential viewers. Creative challenges, such as recreating iconic scenes from the original "Gladiator" or showing off Roman-inspired costumes, have gone viral, drawing in millions of views and interactions. Influencers and TikTok stars have been brought on board to create themed content, further amplifying the film's presence on the platform.

Immersive Experiences: Bringing Rome to Life

One of the standout strategies in the marketing campaign for "Gladiator 2" has been the creation of immersive experiences that transport fans into the world of the film. In key cities around the world, pop-up events have been organized, featuring elaborate set pieces, live performances, and interactive exhibits.

In Los Angeles, a replica of the Colosseum was constructed in a major public space, complete with costumed actors performing gladiatorial combat. Visitors could walk through the arena, take part in sword-fighting workshops, and even try on replicas of the costumes worn by the characters. These events were designed not only to promote the film but also to provide a memorable and engaging experience that fans could share on social media.

In London, a themed escape room was launched, inspired by the political intrigue and conspiracies of ancient Rome. Participants had to solve puzzles and uncover secrets to escape, with the experience tying directly into the plot of "Gladiator 2." This innovative approach not only generated buzz but also deepened the audience's connection to the narrative and themes of the film.

Collaborations and Partnerships: Expanding the Reach

Strategic collaborations and partnerships have been integral to the marketing campaign, expanding the film's reach and tapping into new audiences. One notable partnership has been with historical and cultural institutions, such as the British Museum and the Getty Villa, which have hosted special exhibits on Roman history and the gladiatorial games, featuring artifacts and educational content that tie into the film's themes.

Brands and merchandise collaborations have also played a key role. A luxury watch brand released a limited-edition "Gladiator" series, with designs inspired by Roman armor and symbols. High-end fashion labels have launched clothing lines featuring Roman motifs, while toy companies have produced detailed action figures of the main characters. These partnerships not only generate additional revenue but also keep the film top of mind across various consumer markets.

Influencer Marketing: Harnessing Digital Voices

Influencer marketing has been a cornerstone of the campaign, with influencers across various niches—film critics, history buffs, fashion icons, and fitness gurus—brought on board to create content around "Gladiator 2." These influencers have shared their own takes on the film, whether through in-depth analyses, themed workouts inspired by gladiatorial training, or fashion tips for achieving a Roman-inspired look.

This strategy leverages the trust and reach of influencers to authentically promote the film. By providing influencers with early access to trailers, exclusive interviews, and special behind-the-scenes content, the marketing team has ensured a steady stream of organic and engaging content that reaches a wide audience.

Digital Advertising and Targeted Campaigns

Digital advertising has been meticulously planned and executed, with targeted campaigns across various online platforms. Google Ads, YouTube pre-rolls, and social media advertisements have been tailored to reach specific demographics, from fans of historical dramas to action movie enthusiasts.

Retargeting strategies have been employed to keep the film in front of potential viewers. For instance, those who watched the trailer on YouTube might see follow-up ads on Instagram or Facebook, reminding them of the release date and encouraging them to buy tickets. This multi-platform approach ensures maximum visibility and reinforces the film's presence in the minds of the audience.

Anticipation and Final Push: Countdown to Release

As the release date approaches, the marketing campaign has ramped up with a countdown strategy. Daily content drops, including character posters, final trailers, and exclusive clips, keep the excitement building. Special edition tickets and premiere events are promoted, offering fans the chance to be among the first to see the film.

The final push includes media appearances by the cast and director, interviews on major talk shows, and coverage in entertainment magazines. This blitz of activity ensures that "Gladiator 2" remains a focal point in the cultural conversation, driving home the anticipation and ensuring a strong opening weekend.

Conclusion

The marketing strategies and campaigns for "Gladiator 2" represent a masterclass in modern film promotion. By blending traditional advertising with innovative digital and experiential marketing, the team has crafted a comprehensive approach that engages audiences on multiple levels. From the early teasers that sparked curiosity to the immersive experiences that brought ancient Rome to life, every element of the campaign has been designed to build anticipation and ensure the film's success.

As the world awaits the return to the Colosseum, the meticulous and multi-faceted marketing efforts have laid a solid foundation for "Gladiator 2" to make a triumphant debut. Through a combination of nostalgia, innovation, and audience engagement, the campaign has set the stage for an epic cinematic experience that promises to captivate and inspire.

Marketing Strategies and Campaigns

The marketing strategies and campaigns for "Gladiator 2" are a testament to the art of modern cinematic promotion, weaving a rich tapestry of traditional advertising, immersive experiences, and innovative social media engagement. This multifaceted approach ensures that the anticipation for the film reaches a crescendo, drawing in both die-hard fans of the original and a new generation of viewers. Let's delve into the various elements that compose this masterful campaign, from the tantalizing teasers to the grand promotional events that have captivated audiences worldwide.

Teaser Campaign: Igniting the Flame

The marketing journey for "Gladiator 2" began with a series of enigmatic teasers, strategically released to spark curiosity and rekindle the flames of nostalgia. These short, evocative clips were strategically timed to coincide with major events like the Super Bowl and Comic-Con. Each teaser was a carefully crafted mosaic of visual and auditory elements, designed to evoke the grandeur of ancient Rome and the heroism of Maximus Decimus Meridius.

At the Super Bowl, a 30-second spot aired, showcasing rapid cuts of intense battle scenes and glimpses of the new protagonist, Lucius Verus, set against the backdrop of Hans Zimmer's powerful score. This brief yet impactful teaser immediately sparked conversations, lighting up social media platforms with speculation and excitement. The carefully chosen imagery—Maximus's iconic helmet, the shadowy arches of the Colosseum—served as visual breadcrumbs, leading audiences deeper into the mystery of the sequel.

Full Trailer Launch: A Grand Unveiling

The release of the full trailer was an event unto itself, meticulously planned to maximize impact and reach. Premiered across multiple platforms—YouTube, Instagram, Twitter—the trailer was simultaneously showcased in cinemas ahead of blockbuster movies, ensuring it reached a wide and diverse audience. The trailer's unveiling was accompanied by a live Q&A session with director Ridley Scott and key cast members, streamed on YouTube and Facebook Live. This interactive element allowed fans to engage directly with the creators, deepening their connection to the film.

The trailer itself was a masterclass in cinematic storytelling, opening with a sweeping aerial shot of the Colosseum and a voiceover that set the stage: "Rome stands on the brink, its heart in the hands of a new generation." This line, coupled with visuals of the city's grandeur and decay, established the stakes and immediately drew viewers into the narrative. The trailer balanced quiet, character-driven moments with scenes of epic scale, intercutting political intrigue with visceral combat sequences.

Social Media Campaigns: Digital Engagement

Social media has been a cornerstone of the marketing strategy for "Gladiator 2," with the film's official accounts buzzing with activity. Platforms like Instagram, Twitter, and TikTok have been used to share a steady stream of content, from behind-the-scenes footage and character spotlights to thematic insights and fan interactions.

Instagram, with its visual focus, has been a hub for exclusive images and short video clips. High-quality stills from the film, character portraits, and scenic shots of Rome and the Colosseum have been posted regularly, accompanied by engaging captions and hashtags like #ReturnToTheColosseum and #Gladiator2. Instagram Stories and Reels have been used to share snippets of cast interviews, set tours, and fan reactions, creating a dynamic and interactive experience.

Twitter has served as the platform for real-time updates and fan engagement. The marketing team has orchestrated hashtag campaigns, encouraging fans to share their excitement, theories, and fan art. Regular retweets and replies from the official account have fostered a sense of community and inclusivity, making fans feel like active participants in the film's journey.

TikTok, with its younger demographic and emphasis on short-form video content, has been leveraged to reach a new generation of potential viewers. Creative challenges, such as recreating iconic scenes from the original "Gladiator" or showcasing Roman-inspired costumes, have gone viral, drawing in millions of views and interactions. Influencers and TikTok stars have been brought on board to create themed content, further amplifying the film's presence on the platform.

Immersive Experiences: Bringing Rome to Life

One of the standout strategies in the marketing campaign for "Gladiator 2" has been the creation of immersive experiences that transport fans into the world of the film. In key cities around the world, pop-up events have been organized, featuring elaborate set pieces, live performances, and interactive exhibits.

In Los Angeles, a replica of the Colosseum was constructed in a major public space, complete with costumed actors performing gladiatorial combat. Visitors could walk through the arena, take part in sword-fighting workshops, and even try on replicas of the costumes worn by the characters. These events were designed not only to promote the film but also to provide a memorable and engaging experience that fans could share on social media.

In London, a themed escape room was launched, inspired by the political intrigue and conspiracies of ancient Rome. Participants had to solve puzzles and uncover secrets to escape, with the experience tying directly into the plot of "Gladiator 2." This innovative approach not only generated buzz but also deepened the audience's connection to the narrative and themes of the film.

Collaborations and Partnerships: Expanding the Reach

Strategic collaborations and partnerships have been integral to the marketing campaign, expanding the film's reach and tapping into new audiences. One notable partnership has been with historical and cultural institutions, such as the British Museum and the Getty Villa, which have hosted special exhibits on Roman history and the gladiatorial games, featuring artifacts and educational content that tie into the film's themes.

Brands and merchandise collaborations have also played a key role. A luxury watch brand released a limited-edition "Gladiator" series, with designs inspired by Roman armor and symbols. High-end fashion labels have launched clothing lines featuring Roman motifs, while toy companies have produced detailed action figures of the main characters. These partnerships not only generate additional revenue but also keep the film top of mind across various consumer markets.

Influencer Marketing: Harnessing Digital Voices

Influencer marketing has been a cornerstone of the campaign, with influencers across various niches—film critics, history buffs, fashion icons, and fitness gurus—brought on board to create content around "Gladiator 2." These influencers have shared their own takes on the film, whether through in-depth analyses, themed workouts inspired by gladiatorial training, or fashion tips for achieving a Roman-inspired look.

This strategy leverages the trust and reach of influencers to authentically promote the film. By providing influencers with early access to trailers, exclusive interviews, and special behind-the-scenes content, the marketing team has ensured a steady stream of organic and engaging content that reaches a wide audience.

Digital Advertising and Targeted Campaigns

Digital advertising has been meticulously planned and executed, with targeted campaigns across various online platforms. Google Ads, YouTube pre-rolls, and social media advertisements have been tailored to reach specific demographics, from fans of historical dramas to action movie enthusiasts.

Retargeting strategies have been employed to keep the film in front of potential viewers. For instance, those who watched the trailer on YouTube might see follow-up ads on Instagram or Facebook, reminding them of the release date and encouraging them to buy tickets. This multi-platform approach ensures maximum visibility and reinforces the film's presence in the minds of the audience.

Anticipation and Final Push: Countdown to Release

As the release date approaches, the marketing campaign has ramped up with a countdown strategy. Daily content drops, including character posters, final trailers, and exclusive clips, keep the excitement building. Special edition tickets and premiere events are promoted, offering fans the chance to be among the first to see the film.

The final push includes media appearances by the cast and director, interviews on major talk shows, and coverage in entertainment magazines. This blitz of activity ensures that "Gladiator 2" remains a focal point in the cultural conversation, driving home the anticipation and ensuring a strong opening weekend.

Conclusion

The marketing strategies and campaigns for "Gladiator 2" represent a masterclass in modern film promotion. By blending traditional advertising with innovative digital and experiential marketing, the team has crafted a comprehensive approach that engages audiences on multiple levels. From the early teasers that sparked curiosity to the immersive experiences that brought ancient Rome to life, every element of the campaign has been designed to build anticipation and ensure the film's success.

As the world awaits the return to the Colosseum, the meticulous and multi-faceted marketing efforts have laid a solid foundation for "Gladiator 2" to make a triumphant debut.

Through a combination of nostalgia, innovation, and audience engagement, the campaign has set the stage for an epic cinematic experience that promises to captivate and inspire.

Release Information

Official Release Date

The long-anticipated sequel to Ridley Scott's epic "Gladiator" is set to make a grand return to cinemas under the title "Gladiator 2." Fans and movie enthusiasts around the globe can mark their calendars for this monumental release, scheduled for late 2024. Here's a detailed look at the official release date, the rollout schedule, and the strategic decisions surrounding its premiere.

Official Release Date and Schedule

"Gladiator 2" is slated for an international release on November 15, 2024, which includes major markets such as the United Kingdom. This initial release will be followed by its debut in the United States and Canada a week later, on November 22, 2024. This staggered release strategy is designed to build momentum and maximize global box office returns by generating early reviews and buzz in international markets before hitting North American theaters.

Changes and Adjustments

The film's release date has seen a couple of shifts during its production phase. Initially, there were plans for a simultaneous global release on November 22, 2024. However, the strategy was adjusted to accommodate a more phased rollout, potentially to avoid direct competition with other major releases and to ensure a more sustained promotional campaign.

Interestingly, the release of "Gladiator 2" coincides with the first part of the highly anticipated musical adaptation "Wicked," which will also debut around the same time. This scheduling has led to speculations about a possible "Glicked" phenomenon, similar to the "Barbenheimer" craze of 2023 when "Barbie" and "Oppenheimer" were released on the same weekend. This dual-release scenario aims to draw massive audiences to theaters, creating a blockbuster weekend at the box office.

Strategic Timing

The choice of a late November release places "Gladiator 2" squarely in the middle of the prestigious Oscar season. This timing is strategic, as it aligns with the period when studios release their most ambitious and critically acclaimed films, hoping to garner attention from both audiences and award voters. Given the original "Gladiator's" success at the Academy Awards, there are high expectations for the sequel to follow in its footsteps and possibly secure nominations in multiple categories.

Promotion Leading Up to Release

The marketing campaign for "Gladiator 2" has been meticulously planned to maximize anticipation and engagement. Starting with cryptic teasers and culminating in a full trailer release, the campaign has utilized a blend of traditional and digital marketing strategies. Key promotional activities included:

- **Teaser Campaigns**: Short, evocative teasers were released during major events like the Super Bowl and Comic-Con, featuring iconic imagery and the haunting strains of Hans Zimmer's score. These teasers effectively rekindled interest and speculation about the film.

- **Trailer Releases**: The full trailer was unveiled across multiple platforms, accompanied by live Q&A sessions with Ridley Scott and the main cast. These sessions allowed fans to engage directly with the filmmakers, deepening their connection to the film.

- **Social Media Engagement**: The official social media accounts have been buzzing with activity, sharing behind-the-scenes footage, character spotlights, and thematic insights. Hashtag campaigns like #ReturnToTheColosseum have encouraged fans to share their excitement and theories, creating a vibrant online community.

Final Preparations

As the release date approaches, the final phase of the marketing campaign includes a countdown strategy with daily content drops. Character posters, exclusive clips, and special edition tickets are all part of this final push to maintain high levels of excitement and anticipation.

Media appearances by the cast and director on major talk shows and entertainment platforms are scheduled to keep the film in the public eye. This comprehensive promotional blitz aims to ensure a strong opening weekend, setting the stage for "Gladiator 2" to be both a commercial success and a critical darling.

Conclusion

"Gladiator 2" is poised to be one of the most significant cinematic events of 2024, with its official release dates meticulously chosen to maximize global impact. The combination of a phased international rollout, strategic timing during Oscar season, and a robust marketing campaign all contribute to the heightened anticipation for this epic sequel. As the world prepares to return to the grandeur of the Colosseum and the rich tapestry of ancient Rome, "Gladiator 2" promises to deliver a cinematic experience that honors its legendary predecessor while forging its own path into film history.

Theatrical vs. Streaming Release Plans

In the modern cinematic landscape, the debate between theatrical and streaming releases has become a central issue for studios and filmmakers alike. "Gladiator 2," one of the most anticipated films of 2024, navigates this complex environment with a strategic approach to its distribution. This section will explore the pros and cons of both release strategies, the specific plans for "Gladiator 2," and the expected impact on viewership and revenue.

Theatrical Release: Tradition and Spectacle

Pros:

1. **Cinematic Experience:** The grandeur of "Gladiator 2" demands a big screen. The Colosseum battles, the sweeping landscapes of ancient Rome, and Hans Zimmer's immersive score are designed to be experienced in a theater. The impact of these elements is amplified in a cinema setting, providing an experience that is hard to replicate at home.

2. **Box Office Revenue:** A successful theatrical release can generate substantial box office revenue. The original "Gladiator" grossed over $460 million worldwide. With the sequel, the studio hopes to replicate or exceed this success, leveraging the global fanbase and the film's built-in audience.

3. **Cultural Event:** Theatrical releases often become cultural events. Opening weekends create buzz and excitement, driving word-of-mouth marketing. Films like "Gladiator 2" can dominate social conversations, media coverage, and fan activities, reinforcing their status as must-see events.

4. **Awards Consideration:** Theatrical releases are still the preferred format for many prestigious awards, including the Oscars. A strong theatrical run can

bolster a film's chances during awards season, enhancing its prestige and longevity.

Cons:

1. **High Costs:** Theatrical releases involve significant costs, including marketing, distribution, and exhibition fees. The pandemic has also introduced uncertainties, with fluctuating theater attendance and potential restrictions affecting box office performance.

2. **Competition:** The theatrical landscape is competitive, with multiple releases vying for audience attention. "Gladiator 2" will be competing with other major films, such as the musical adaptation "Wicked," which could split the audience and impact box office results.

Streaming Release: Accessibility and Reach

Pros:

1. **Wide Accessibility:** Streaming platforms provide unparalleled accessibility. Audiences worldwide can watch "Gladiator 2" from the comfort of their homes, increasing potential viewership. This is particularly beneficial for audiences who may not have access to theaters or prefer home viewing.

2. **Subscriber Growth:** Releasing a major film like "Gladiator 2" on a streaming platform can drive subscriber growth. Exclusive content is a powerful incentive for new subscribers, contributing to the platform's long-term revenue.

3. **Data and Analytics:** Streaming platforms offer detailed data and analytics on viewership patterns, engagement, and demographics. This information can be invaluable for future marketing and production decisions.

4. **Flexibility:** Streaming releases offer flexibility in terms of viewing times and formats. Audiences can

watch at their convenience, which can enhance the overall viewing experience and increase engagement.

Cons:

1. **Revenue Model:** While streaming can generate significant revenue through subscriptions, it often lacks the immediate financial impact of a theatrical box office run. The revenue model is also dependent on subscriber retention, which can be challenging to sustain.

2. **Piracy Risks:** Streaming releases are more vulnerable to piracy. Once a film is available online, unauthorized copies can quickly spread, potentially impacting revenue and viewership.

3. **Experience Quality:** The home viewing experience, despite advancements in home theater technology, cannot match the immersive quality of a cinema. The visual and auditory impact of "Gladiator 2" may be diminished on smaller screens and standard audio systems.

Hybrid Release Strategy

Given the pros and cons of both theatrical and streaming releases, many studios have adopted a hybrid approach. This strategy combines an initial theatrical release with a subsequent streaming debut, aiming to maximize both revenue streams and audience reach.

For "Gladiator 2," the studio has opted for a traditional theatrical release followed by a streaming debut. The film will premiere in theaters worldwide on November 22, 2024, with an initial rollout in the UK on November 15, 2024. This staggered release strategy is designed to build momentum and maximize box office returns before the film becomes available on streaming platforms.

Theatrical Window:

The film will have an exclusive theatrical window of approximately 45 days. This period is critical for generating box office revenue and leveraging the cultural event status of the film. The studio is banking on the appeal of the cinematic experience to draw audiences to theaters, capitalizing on the immersive qualities that a film like "Gladiator 2" offers.

Streaming Debut:

Following the theatrical window, "Gladiator 2" will be available for streaming on a major platform, likely Paramount+, given the studio's existing distribution partnerships. This release will cater to audiences who prefer home viewing and those who missed the theatrical run. By staggering the release, the studio aims to tap into the strengths of both models, ensuring that "Gladiator 2" reaches the widest possible audience.

Expected Impact on Viewership and Revenue

Viewership:

The hybrid release strategy is expected to maximize viewership. The initial theatrical run will attract traditional cinema-goers and fans of the original film, generating significant box office revenue. The subsequent streaming release will broaden the audience, appealing to those who prefer the convenience and accessibility of home viewing.

By combining both platforms, "Gladiator 2" can engage different demographics and viewing preferences, ensuring that the film remains a topic of discussion across various media and social platforms. This approach also allows the studio to extend the film's lifecycle, maintaining relevance and engagement well beyond the initial release period.

Revenue:

The hybrid model aims to balance immediate box office returns with long-term streaming revenue. The theatrical release will provide a substantial upfront revenue boost, essential for recouping production and marketing costs. The streaming debut will generate ongoing revenue through subscriptions and digital purchases.

This strategy also mitigates risks associated with either model. If theatrical attendance is lower than expected due to external factors like a pandemic resurgence or competing releases, the streaming release can compensate by reaching a broader audience. Conversely, a strong theatrical performance can enhance the film's profile, driving higher engagement and subscriptions when it becomes available for streaming.

Conclusion

The release strategy for "Gladiator 2" reflects a nuanced understanding of the contemporary cinematic landscape. By leveraging the strengths of both theatrical and streaming platforms, the studio aims to maximize viewership and revenue while delivering an epic cinematic experience. The traditional theatrical release, followed by a strategic streaming debut, ensures that "Gladiator 2" can captivate audiences worldwide, honoring its legacy while embracing modern viewing habits.

As the world eagerly awaits the return to the Colosseum, the release strategy for "Gladiator 2" promises to deliver an unforgettable journey through ancient Rome, tailored to the diverse preferences of today's global audience.

Premiere Events and Expectations

As "Gladiator 2" gears up for its grand release, the anticipation surrounding its premiere events is reaching a fever pitch. These events promise to be as grand and spectacular as the film itself, drawing in fans, celebrities, and media from around the world. The premieres will serve as both a celebration of the film's release and a testament to its cultural impact. Here's a detailed look at the planned events, star appearances, and the expected reception for "Gladiator 2."

Planned Premiere Events

World Premiere in Rome:

Fittingly, the world premiere of "Gladiator 2" will take place in Rome, the heart of the ancient empire that serves as the film's setting. The premiere is set to be held at the historic Teatro dell'Opera di Roma, a venue known for its opulence and grandeur. This choice of location not only pays homage to the film's historical roots but also provides a stunning backdrop that enhances the event's visual and thematic resonance.

The red carpet event will feature an elaborate setup that includes replicas of Roman architecture, complete with columns, statues, and even a mini-Colosseum. Guests will be greeted by actors dressed in traditional Roman attire, creating an immersive experience that transports attendees back to ancient times. This premiere is expected to be a star-studded affair, with the cast and crew, alongside notable figures from the entertainment industry and dignitaries.

Hollywood Premiere:

Following the Rome premiere, a second major event will take place in Hollywood, at the iconic TCL Chinese Theatre. This venue, steeped in cinematic history, is the perfect location for a film of "Gladiator 2's" magnitude. The Hollywood premiere will feature a more modern red carpet setup, blending elements of ancient Rome with contemporary Hollywood glamour.

The event will include a pre-screening reception, where guests can mingle and enjoy themed cocktails and hors d'oeuvres inspired by Roman cuisine. Interactive exhibits will showcase costumes, props, and behind-the-scenes footage, offering fans an exclusive glimpse into the making of the film. The Hollywood premiere is expected to attract a wide array of celebrities, media personalities, and influencers, further amplifying the film's visibility and buzz.

International Premieres:

In addition to the Rome and Hollywood events, "Gladiator 2" will have several international premieres in key markets such as London, Paris, and Tokyo. These premieres will be tailored to their respective locales, incorporating cultural elements that resonate with local audiences while maintaining the film's thematic essence. Each event will feature appearances by local celebrities and influencers, enhancing the film's global appeal and reach.

Star Appearances

The premiere events will be graced by the film's stellar cast, including Paul Mescal (Lucius Verus), Barry Keoghan (Sejanus), and Connie Nielsen (Lucilla), among others. Director Ridley Scott will also be present, providing insights into the making of the film and his vision for the sequel.

Paul Mescal, the rising star who plays Lucius Verus, is expected to be a focal point of media attention. His recent performances have garnered critical acclaim, and his role in "Gladiator 2" is anticipated to elevate his status in Hollywood further. Barry Keoghan, known for his intense and compelling performances, will also draw significant interest, particularly regarding his portrayal of the film's antagonist, Sejanus.

Connie Nielsen's return as Lucilla will be another highlight, offering continuity between the original film and the sequel. Her presence on the red carpet will be a nostalgic reminder of the original "Gladiator" and its lasting legacy.

Anticipated Reception

The reception for "Gladiator 2" is expected to be overwhelmingly positive, given the legacy of the original film and the talent involved in the sequel. Early buzz from industry insiders suggests that the film stays true to the spirit of its predecessor while introducing fresh elements that will captivate both old fans and new audiences.

Critical Expectations:

Critics are likely to focus on several key aspects, including the film's narrative, visual effects, and performances. Ridley Scott's direction, known for its epic scale and meticulous attention to detail, will be closely scrutinized. The return of Hans Zimmer to score the film will also be a significant point of interest, with many anticipating a soundtrack that rivals the original's iconic music.

Audience Anticipation:

Fans of the original "Gladiator" have high expectations for the sequel, hoping for a film that honors the legacy of Maximus while introducing compelling new characters and storylines. The trailers and promotional materials have already generated significant excitement, with discussions and theories proliferating across social media platforms.

The immersive premiere events are expected to enhance this anticipation, creating memorable experiences that fans will share widely, further fueling the film's buzz. The strategic release of exclusive content, such as behind-the-scenes footage and cast interviews, will keep the momentum going, ensuring that "Gladiator 2" remains a topic of conversation leading up to and beyond its release.

Conclusion

The premiere events for "Gladiator 2" promise to be grand, immersive celebrations that honor the film's epic scope and historical roots. From the world premiere in Rome to the glamorous Hollywood event and international showcases, each premiere is meticulously planned to maximize impact and engagement.

Star appearances, particularly those of Paul Mescal, Barry Keoghan, and Connie Nielsen, will draw significant media attention, while the presence of Ridley Scott and Hans Zimmer will add further prestige to the events. The anticipated reception, buoyed by positive early buzz and high expectations from fans and critics alike, suggests that "Gladiator 2" will make a powerful debut, solidifying its place as one of the most significant cinematic releases of 2024.

As the world eagerly awaits the film's release, the premiere events will not only celebrate the film but also create a lasting impact, ensuring that "Gladiator 2" is remembered as a monumental cinematic experience.

Fan Reactions and Expectations

Social Media Buzz

As the release date for "Gladiator 2" approaches, social media platforms are ablaze with excitement and speculation. Fans of the original film and new viewers alike have taken to Twitter, Instagram, TikTok, and Reddit to share their thoughts, theories, and anticipations for Ridley Scott's epic sequel. The online buzz reflects a vibrant tapestry of emotions, from nostalgia and excitement to curiosity and impatience. Let's delve into the online discussions, trends, and fan reactions that have shaped the social media landscape around "Gladiator 2."

Twitter: The Epicenter of Instant Reactions

On Twitter, the hashtag #Gladiator2 has been trending frequently, often accompanied by gifs, clips from the original movie, and enthusiastic comments from fans. The platform's real-time nature makes it ideal for spontaneous reactions, especially following the release of trailers and teasers. Fans have been quick to express their excitement over the return of familiar characters and the introduction of new ones.

One user tweeted, "Just saw the #Gladiator2 trailer and I'm SHOOK! Paul Mescal as Lucius looks incredible, and Barry Keoghan as Sejanus? This is going to be EPIC!" Another fan echoed this sentiment, writing, "The cinematography and score in the #Gladiator2 trailer gave me chills. Can't wait to see it on the big screen!"

Discussions on Twitter also frequently revolve around the soundtrack, with many users expressing their anticipation for Hans Zimmer's return. "Hans Zimmer back for #Gladiator2 is the best news! The music from the original still gives me goosebumps. Ready for round two!" tweeted an excited fan.

Instagram: Visual Storytelling and Behind-the-Scenes Insights

Instagram has become a hub for visual storytelling, with the film's official account sharing a plethora of behind-the-scenes photos, character posters, and short video clips. These posts are often accompanied by engaging captions that provide insights into the filmmaking process and the characters' journeys.

Fans have been particularly drawn to the character portraits, which offer a closer look at the actors in their Roman attire. "Paul Mescal looks so regal as Lucius! The costumes and makeup are just perfection," commented one user. Another fan posted, "Barry Keoghan's eyes are so intense as Sejanus. You can tell he's going to be a compelling villain."

Instagram Stories and Reels have also been utilized effectively to share snippets of cast interviews, set tours, and interactive Q&A sessions. These short, engaging pieces of content keep the excitement building and encourage fans to share their own reactions and theories.

TikTok: Creative Fan Engagement and Viral Trends

TikTok, with its emphasis on short-form video content, has seen a surge in creative fan engagement. Users have been recreating iconic scenes from the original "Gladiator" and speculating on plot details for the sequel. One popular trend involves fans dressing up in Roman-inspired costumes and acting out scenes, often with a humorous twist.

The hashtag #Gladiator2Challenge has gained traction, encouraging users to share their best gladiatorial poses or reenactments. One viral video features a group of friends staging a mini gladiator fight in their backyard, complete with makeshift props and dramatic slow-motion effects. "We might not be in the Colosseum, but we can still fight like gladiators! #Gladiator2Challenge" reads the caption.

TikTok influencers have also joined the buzz, creating content that ranges from deep dives into Roman history to fitness routines inspired by gladiatorial training. These influencers, with their large followings, have helped amplify the film's presence on the platform and engage a younger audience.

Reddit: In-Depth Discussions and Fan Theories

On Reddit, the r/movies and r/Gladiator2 subreddits have become hotspots for in-depth discussions and fan theories. Reddit's format allows for longer, more detailed posts and comments, providing a space for fans to delve into the nuances of the film's plot and characters.

One popular thread explores the potential storyline of "Gladiator 2," with users speculating on Lucius's journey and Sejanus's role as the antagonist. "I think Lucius will struggle with his identity and the legacy of Maximus. Sejanus might try to manipulate him to seize power," suggests one user. Another commenter adds, "There's definitely going to be a big showdown in the Colosseum. Ridley Scott knows how to stage epic battles!"

Another thread discusses the historical accuracy of the film, with history buffs weighing in on the depiction of Roman culture and politics. "The attention to detail in the set design and costumes is impressive. I hope they stick close to historical facts while still delivering a compelling story," writes one user.

Anticipated Reception and Fan Expectations

The overall reception on social media indicates high expectations for "Gladiator 2." Fans are eager to see how the film balances homage to the original with new elements that expand the story. There is a palpable sense of excitement for the performances, particularly those of Paul Mescal and Barry Keoghan, as well as the direction of Ridley Scott and the music of Hans Zimmer.

Fans are also hopeful that "Gladiator 2" will deliver the same emotional and visual impact as its predecessor. The anticipation is not just for the spectacle of the battles but also for the depth of the characters and the narrative. "I'm looking forward to seeing Lucius's character development and how he deals with the shadow of Maximus," writes one Twitter user.

Conclusion

The social media buzz surrounding "Gladiator 2" is a testament to the film's enduring legacy and the excitement it has generated among fans. Platforms like Twitter, Instagram, TikTok, and Reddit have become vibrant arenas for discussions, creative expressions, and fan theories. As the release date draws nearer, this buzz is only expected to grow, fueled by the strategic marketing campaigns and the genuine enthusiasm of the global fanbase.

The varied reactions and interactions highlight the multifaceted appeal of "Gladiator 2," promising a film that not only honors its iconic predecessor but also introduces new layers of storytelling and cinematic experience. As fans continue to share their thoughts and anticipations, the world awaits the grand return to the Colosseum, ready to be entertained once more.

Early Reviews and Critiques

As the curtain rises on "Gladiator 2," the flood of early reviews and critiques from both critics and audiences has started to paint a vivid picture of the film's reception. With the weight of its legendary predecessor on its shoulders, the sequel has sparked a wide range of opinions, blending high praise with pointed critiques. This section delves into the initial reactions, highlighting key points of acclaim and criticism to provide a comprehensive overview of the film's early reception.

Critical Acclaim: The Triumphs

Visual and Cinematic Brilliance: One of the most universally praised aspects of "Gladiator 2" is its stunning visual and cinematic achievement. Critics have lauded Ridley Scott's masterful direction, which brings ancient Rome to life with breathtaking detail. The film's use of cutting-edge CGI and practical effects to recreate the grandeur of the Colosseum and the Roman landscape has been described as a visual feast. RogerEbert.com noted, "Scott's meticulous attention to historical detail, combined with the latest visual effects, creates a vividly immersive experience that transports audiences back to the glory and brutality of ancient Rome."

Paul Mescal's Performance: Paul Mescal's portrayal of Lucius Verus has been a standout, earning high praise from critics for his compelling and nuanced performance. Mescal brings a depth to the character that reflects both the legacy of Maximus and the personal struggles of a young leader in a turbulent era. The Hollywood Reporter commented, "Mescal's Lucius is a powerful blend of vulnerability and strength, a character torn between his heritage and his destiny. His performance is both commanding and deeply human, anchoring the film's epic narrative with emotional gravitas."

Score by Hans Zimmer: Hans Zimmer's return as the composer for "Gladiator 2" has been met with widespread acclaim. His score, a blend of haunting motifs from the original and new, powerful themes, has been praised for enhancing the film's emotional and dramatic arcs. Variety highlighted, "Zimmer's music weaves a rich tapestry that echoes the past while propelling the story forward, each note resonating with the grandeur and pathos that defined the original score."

Audience Feedback: The Enthusiasts

Nostalgia and Continuity: Fans of the original "Gladiator" have expressed deep appreciation for the sequel's respectful nods to its predecessor. The careful integration of iconic elements, such as Maximus's legacy and familiar musical motifs, has resonated strongly with long-time fans. On social media platforms, numerous fans have shared their emotional reactions to these callbacks. A Twitter user wrote, "The moment I heard the familiar strains of Maximus's theme, I was instantly transported back to my first viewing of Gladiator. It's a perfect blend of old and new."

Action Sequences: The action sequences in "Gladiator 2" have garnered enthusiastic praise for their intensity and choreography. The Colosseum battles, in particular, have been highlighted for their visceral energy and realism. On Reddit, fans have discussed the thrill of the combat scenes, with one user noting, "The gladiatorial fights are incredibly well-executed, with a level of detail and brutality that feels authentic. Each battle is a mini-epic in itself."

Character Development: Many viewers have appreciated the depth of character development in the sequel, particularly the growth and transformation of Lucius. The film's exploration of his internal conflicts and leadership challenges has struck a chord with audiences. An Instagram fan account commented, "Lucius's journey from a young boy in the shadow of Maximus to a leader in his own right is beautifully portrayed. It's a compelling character arc that adds layers to the story."

Critiques and Mixed Reactions

Pacing Issues: Some critics and viewers have pointed out pacing issues in the film, particularly in its middle act. The transitions between the political intrigue and the action sequences have been described as uneven, leading to moments where the narrative momentum lags. The Guardian mentioned, "While the film's opening and closing acts are gripping, there are stretches in the middle that feel slow and overstuffed, detracting from the overall flow."

Over-Reliance on Nostalgia: A few critiques have noted that "Gladiator 2" leans heavily on the nostalgia for its predecessor, sometimes at the expense of developing its own identity. These critics argue that while the callbacks to the original are effective, they occasionally overshadow the new elements of the story. IndieWire remarked, "The film walks a fine line between homage and repetition. At times, it feels as though it's trying too hard to replicate the magic of the first Gladiator, rather than forging its own path."

Character Utilization: Some audience members have expressed disappointment over the utilization of certain characters, feeling that key figures like Sejanus did not receive enough screen time or depth. Discussions on fan forums have highlighted this as a missed opportunity, with one user on a movie subreddit stating, "Barry Keoghan's Sejanus had so much potential, but his character arc felt rushed and underdeveloped. I wanted more from his storyline."

Overall Reception

Despite these critiques, the overall reception of "Gladiator 2" has been largely positive. The film's ability to blend epic action with emotional storytelling has resonated with many, and its visual and auditory elements have been universally praised. Early reviews from major publications have been favorable, with many highlighting the film's ambitious scope and strong performances.

Metacritic and Rotten Tomatoes Scores: As of the latest updates, "Gladiator 2" holds a commendable score on Metacritic, reflecting generally favorable reviews from critics. Rotten Tomatoes also shows a high audience score, indicating strong viewer approval. These metrics suggest that while the film has its flaws, it succeeds in delivering a powerful and engaging cinematic experience.

Conclusion

The early reviews and critiques of "Gladiator 2" paint a picture of a film that ambitiously strives to honor its legendary predecessor while carving out its own place in the cinematic landscape. With standout performances, particularly from Paul Mescal, a masterful score by Hans Zimmer, and visually stunning direction by Ridley Scott, the film offers much to admire.

However, it is not without its shortcomings. Issues with pacing, an over-reliance on nostalgia, and underutilized characters have been pointed out by both critics and audiences. Despite these criticisms, the overall reception has been positive, indicating that "Gladiator 2" succeeds in recapturing the epic spirit of the original while delivering a new and compelling story.

As the conversation continues to unfold on social media and in critical circles, "Gladiator 2" stands as a testament to the enduring legacy of Maximus and the timeless allure of the Colosseum. The world awaits with bated breath, ready to be entertained once more by the spectacle and drama of ancient Rome.

Fan Art and Community Engagement

As "Gladiator 2" gears up for its release, the fervor within the fan community has manifested in various forms of creative expression and interactive engagement. From stunning fan art to immersive community events, the anticipation for the sequel has inspired a vibrant and dynamic fan culture. This section explores the notable fan creations, community-driven activities, and the overall impact on fan culture surrounding "Gladiator 2."

Notable Fan Art: Visual Homages

One of the most striking ways fans have expressed their excitement for "Gladiator 2" is through fan art. Platforms like Instagram, DeviantArt, and Twitter are brimming with illustrations, paintings, and digital art that pay homage to the beloved characters and epic scenes from the films.

Lucius and Maximus: A Legacy in Art

A recurring theme in fan art is the depiction of Lucius Verus alongside the iconic Maximus Decimus Meridius. Artists have creatively interpreted the bond between the two characters, highlighting Lucius's evolution from a boy in the original film to a leader in the sequel. For instance, a stunning digital painting by @ArtByNia on Instagram portrays Lucius standing resolutely with Maximus's shadow looming behind him, symbolizing the enduring influence of Maximus's legacy.

Epic Battle Scenes

Fans have also focused on the epic battle scenes that define the "Gladiator" series. On DeviantArt, user GladiatorFanatic has created a series of intricate illustrations capturing the intensity of gladiatorial combat, complete with historically accurate armor and weaponry. These pieces not only showcase the artist's skill but also reflect a deep appreciation for the film's historical setting and action-packed narrative.

Character Portraits

Character portraits are another popular subject among fan

artists. Barry Keoghan's Sejanus has inspired numerous works, often emphasizing his cunning and menacing presence. An example is a portrait by @TheRomanArtist on Twitter, which captures Sejanus with piercing eyes and a sinister smirk, rendered in a dark, moody palette that hints at his role as the antagonist.

Community Events: Bringing Fans Together

The anticipation for "Gladiator 2" has also sparked a series of community events, both online and offline, that bring fans together to celebrate their shared enthusiasm.

Virtual Watch Parties

In the lead-up to the sequel's release, virtual watch parties for the original "Gladiator" have become a popular activity. Platforms like Discord and Zoom host these events, where fans gather to watch and discuss the film in real-time. These watch parties often include interactive elements, such as trivia contests and live commentary, enhancing the communal experience. For instance, the "Gladiator Fan Club" on Discord recently hosted a marathon event, complete with themed virtual backgrounds and custom emojis inspired by the film.

Fan Conventions and Panels

At various fan conventions, special panels dedicated to "Gladiator 2" have been organized. These panels feature discussions with historians, film critics, and sometimes even cast members, offering insights into the making of the film and its historical context. At the recent Comic-Con, a "Gladiator 2" panel drew a packed audience, where attendees participated in a Q&A session with the film's production team, gaining exclusive behind-the-scenes knowledge.

Cosplay Contests

Cosplay contests are another highlight of community engagement, with fans donning elaborate costumes inspired by characters from both "Gladiator" films. These contests often take place at conventions and fan gatherings, where participants showcase their creativity and craftsmanship. The winner of a recent cosplay contest at Dragon Con, dressed as Lucilla, impressed judges with an intricately detailed Roman gown and historically accurate accessories.

Overall Impact on Fan Culture

The excitement surrounding "Gladiator 2" has not only rekindled interest in the original film but also spurred a broader engagement with Roman history and culture.

Educational Outreach

Some fan groups have taken the opportunity to combine their love for the film with educational outreach. The "Ancient Rome Enthusiasts" Facebook group, for example, regularly posts educational content about Roman history, tying in aspects of the "Gladiator" films. These posts include detailed articles about the real Colosseum, gladiatorial games, and the historical figures that inspired the characters. This blend of entertainment and education has enriched the fan experience, providing a deeper appreciation for the film's historical context.

Charity and Fundraising

In a heartwarming twist, some fan activities have also focused on charitable causes. Inspired by the themes of bravery and justice in "Gladiator," fans have organized fundraising events for various charities. One notable initiative is the "Gladiator Run," a virtual marathon where participants run or walk in Roman-themed attire to raise money for veterans' organizations. This event, promoted through social media, has seen significant participation and has raised substantial funds for its cause.

Social Media Campaigns

The role of social media in sustaining and amplifying fan engagement cannot be overstated. Hashtags like #Gladiator2Art and #Gladiator2Hype have trended multiple times, with fans sharing their creations and speculations. Twitter polls,

Instagram challenges, and TikTok trends have all contributed to a lively and interactive fan culture. These platforms have become spaces where fans not only express their excitement but also connect with like-minded individuals, fostering a global community united by their love for "Gladiator."

Conclusion

The fan art and community engagement surrounding "Gladiator 2" exemplify the profound impact the film has on its audience. Through creative expressions and communal activities, fans have transformed their anticipation into a vibrant cultural phenomenon. The various forms of engagement, from stunning artworks and cosplay to educational initiatives and charity events, reflect a deep connection to the film's themes and characters.

As the release date for "Gladiator 2" approaches, the excitement within the fan community continues to build. This wave of enthusiasm not only honors the legacy of the original film but also paves the way for the sequel to make a significant cultural impact. Through their passion and creativity, fans have created a rich, multifaceted culture that celebrates the epic spirit of "Gladiator" and eagerly awaits its triumphant return.

Impact on Pop Culture
The Influence of the Original 'Gladiator'

When "Gladiator" was released in 2000, it was more than just a film; it was a cultural phenomenon that left an indelible mark on the pop culture landscape. Directed by Ridley Scott and starring Russell Crowe as the stoic yet impassioned Maximus Decimus Meridius, the film not only captivated audiences with its epic storytelling and visceral combat scenes but also revitalized interest in historical epics. Its influence extended far beyond the silver screen, permeating various facets of entertainment, fashion, language, and even politics. This section explores the profound impact of "Gladiator" on pop culture, its significance in the film industry, and its lasting legacy.

Revitalizing the Historical Epic

Before "Gladiator," the historical epic genre was largely considered a relic of the past, with its heyday in the 1950s and 1960s through films like "Ben-Hur" and "Spartacus." The genre had fallen out of favor, deemed too costly and ambitious for modern Hollywood. However, "Gladiator" changed all that. Its critical and commercial success, grossing over $460 million worldwide, proved that audiences still craved grand narratives set against the backdrop of history.

Ridley Scott's meticulous attention to historical detail and his innovative use of CGI to recreate the grandeur of ancient Rome set a new standard for the genre. The film's success paved the way for a resurgence of historical epics, inspiring a slew of films and television series that sought to capture the same blend of action, drama, and historical authenticity. Movies like "Troy" (2004), "Kingdom of Heaven" (2005), and "300" (2006) owe a debt to "Gladiator" for reigniting interest in epic storytelling.

Cultural Significance and Quotability

"Gladiator" became a cultural touchstone, with its characters and dialogue entering the public lexicon. The film's lines, particularly Maximus's iconic "Are you not entertained?" have been quoted, parodied, and referenced countless times across various media. This line, delivered with fierce intensity by Russell Crowe, encapsulated the film's central theme of personal honor versus public spectacle and has since become a shorthand for questioning the value of entertainment.

The film's depiction of the gladiatorial games also sparked renewed interest in ancient Roman culture. Schools and universities saw an uptick in enrollments in classical studies and courses on Roman history, as students were inspired by the film to learn more about the era. Documentaries and books exploring the historical accuracy of the film and the real-life gladiators also surged in popularity.

Influence on the Film Industry

"Gladiator" had a significant impact on the film industry, particularly in how historical epics were produced and marketed. The film's success demonstrated that there was still a viable market for large-scale historical dramas, leading studios to invest in similar projects. Its blend of practical effects and groundbreaking CGI to recreate ancient Rome was revolutionary, setting a new benchmark for visual effects in historical films.

Moreover, "Gladiator" revitalized the career of Ridley Scott, establishing him as one of the foremost directors of epic cinema. The film also catapulted Russell Crowe to A-list status, earning him an Academy Award for Best Actor and solidifying his place in Hollywood. The film's critical success, winning five Oscars including Best Picture, further cemented its legacy as a modern classic.

Fashion and Aesthetic Influence

The influence of "Gladiator" extended into the world of fashion and aesthetics. The film's costume design, characterized by its detailed and authentic Roman attire, inspired fashion designers to incorporate elements of ancient Roman clothing into their collections. Gladiator sandals, with their distinctive strappy design, became a popular trend in women's footwear following the film's release.

The film's visual style, with its use of earthy tones and dramatic lighting, influenced advertising and music videos, as creators sought to evoke the same epic and timeless quality. The rugged, muscular physique of Russell Crowe's Maximus also set a new standard for male beauty in Hollywood, with many actors adopting similar workout regimens to achieve the "Gladiator" look.

Impact on Language and Expression

The language of "Gladiator" permeated everyday speech, with lines from the film becoming part of common parlance. Phrases like "strength and honor," "at my signal, unleash hell," and "what we do in life, echoes in eternity" have been used in various contexts, from motivational speeches to political rhetoric. These lines, with their poetic resonance and philosophical depth, encapsulate the film's themes of duty, legacy, and the human condition.

The film's dialogue has also been referenced and parodied in television shows, films, and even political speeches. For instance, during the 2008 U.S. presidential campaign, then-Senator John McCain used the line "Are you not entertained?" to critique the media's focus on sensationalism over substantive issues, demonstrating the film's reach into political discourse.

Lasting Legacy and Continued Relevance

Two decades after its release, "Gladiator" remains a seminal film with a lasting legacy. Its influence is evident in the continued popularity of historical dramas and epic storytelling in both film and television. The success of series like "Game of Thrones" and "Vikings" can be traced back to the groundwork laid by "Gladiator," with their emphasis on complex characters, intricate political plots, and grand battle sequences.

The film's themes of honor, revenge, and the quest for justice resonate with contemporary audiences, making it timeless in its appeal. "Gladiator" has inspired numerous academic studies and scholarly articles examining its historical accuracy, narrative structure, and cultural impact, further cementing its status as a modern classic.

In addition, the upcoming release of "Gladiator 2" demonstrates the enduring appeal of the original film. The excitement and anticipation surrounding the sequel reflect the deep connection that audiences still have with the story and characters introduced in the first film. The legacy of Maximus Decimus Meridius lives on, continuing to inspire and entertain new generations.

Conclusion

"Gladiator" is more than just a film; it is a cultural milestone that has left an indelible mark on pop culture. Its revitalization of the historical epic genre, significant impact on the film industry, and pervasive influence on fashion, language, and cultural discourse underscore its status as a modern classic. As we await the release of "Gladiator 2," the legacy of the original film continues to resonate, reminding us of the power of cinema to transport, inspire, and entertain. The story of Maximus Decimus Meridius, with its timeless themes and epic scope, will undoubtedly echo in eternity.

Predicted Cultural Impact of 'Gladiator 2'

As we stand on the precipice of the release of "Gladiator 2," the sequel to one of the most iconic films of the early 21st century, the anticipation is palpable. Ridley Scott's return to the world of ancient Rome, combined with a fresh cast and a continuation of a beloved story, promises to create a significant cultural ripple. This speculative exploration will delve into the potential influences "Gladiator 2" might have on the film industry, pop culture, and audiences, painting a picture of its possible impact.

Reinvigorating the Historical Epic

"Gladiator 2" is poised to once again breathe life into the historical epic genre, a genre that "Gladiator" itself revived in 2000. The sequel is expected to set a new standard for historical dramas, leveraging advanced CGI and practical effects to recreate the grandeur of ancient Rome with unprecedented detail and realism.

Industry Influence:

- **Technological Advancements:** Just as the original film set new benchmarks for visual effects and set design, "Gladiator 2" is likely to push the boundaries of cinematic technology. With advances in CGI and motion capture, the film will offer a more immersive and visually stunning depiction of ancient Rome. This technological leap could inspire other filmmakers to explore historical settings with renewed vigor, utilizing the latest tools to bring their visions to life.

- **Budget and Production Scale:** High-budget historical epics may see a resurgence, with studios more willing to invest in large-scale productions that promise high returns. The success of "Gladiator 2" could reassure studios that there is a substantial audience for well-crafted historical dramas, leading to a wave of similar projects in the pipeline.

Shaping Pop Culture and Fashion

"Gladiator 2" will likely make a substantial mark on pop culture, influencing everything from fashion trends to language and societal attitudes.

Fashion Trends:

- **Roman-Inspired Designs:** The film's costume design, rooted in the elaborate attire of ancient Rome, will likely inspire fashion designers. Expect to see elements like gladiator sandals, togas, and Roman jewelry making a comeback on runways and in retail stores. The aesthetic of "Gladiator 2" could lead to a renaissance of classical influences in contemporary fashion, blending historical elements with modern sensibilities.

- **Fitness and Physique:** The portrayal of gladiators and their rigorous training might influence fitness trends. Workout programs inspired by the physical regimens of ancient warriors could become popular, promoting a blend of strength, agility, and endurance training that mirrors the preparation of the film's characters.

Language and Quotability:

- **Iconic Lines:** Much like its predecessor, "Gladiator 2" is expected to contribute memorable lines to the cultural lexicon. Phrases from the film will likely be quoted in various contexts, from motivational speeches to casual conversations. These lines can become shorthand for broader concepts, reflecting themes of honor, bravery, and resilience.

Audience Engagement and Community

The film's release will likely foster a vibrant community of fans, engaging in discussions, creating content, and participating in events that celebrate the world of "Gladiator."

Fan Art and Fiction:

- **Creative Expression:** Inspired by the film's rich narrative and characters, fans will produce a plethora of fan art, fan fiction, and other creative works. Platforms like DeviantArt, Tumblr, and Instagram will be filled with visual and literary tributes, extending the story of "Gladiator 2" into the realms of personal interpretation and expansion.

- **Community Events:** Online and offline communities will organize events such as watch parties, discussion panels, and cosplay contests. These events will bring fans together, fostering a sense of camaraderie and shared passion for the world Ridley Scott has created.

Educational Impact:

- **Historical Interest:** "Gladiator 2" will spark renewed interest in ancient Roman history. Educational institutions might see an uptick in enrollment for courses related to Roman culture, history, and archaeology. Documentaries, books, and articles exploring the historical accuracy of the film's depiction will proliferate, contributing to a deeper public understanding of the era.

Societal Reflections and Philosophical Themes

"Gladiator 2" is expected to explore themes that resonate with contemporary audiences, reflecting societal issues and philosophical questions that transcend time.

Themes of Power and Corruption:

- **Political Parallels:** The film's exploration of power dynamics, corruption, and the struggle for justice will resonate with modern audiences, drawing parallels to contemporary political landscapes. Discussions and analyses will likely emerge, comparing the film's narrative to current events and societal structures.

- **Personal Honor and Legacy:** The protagonist's journey, mirroring that of Maximus, will delve into the concepts of personal honor, duty, and legacy. These themes will prompt viewers to reflect on their own lives and the values they hold dear, fostering a deeper engagement with the story beyond mere entertainment.

Cultural Dialogue:

- **Ethical Considerations:** The depiction of gladiatorial combat and the moral dilemmas faced by the characters will spark debates about ethics, violence, and the nature of entertainment. These discussions will extend into various media, including podcasts, academic journals, and social commentary platforms, contributing to an ongoing cultural dialogue.

Conclusion

"Gladiator 2" is poised to leave a profound impact on pop culture, much like its predecessor did two decades ago. By reinvigorating the historical epic genre, influencing fashion and language, fostering vibrant fan communities, and prompting societal reflections, the film will extend its reach far beyond the silver screen. As audiences around the world prepare to re-enter the world of ancient Rome, "Gladiator 2" stands ready to not only entertain but also inspire and provoke thought, ensuring its legacy as a cultural touchstone for years to come.

Legacy and Future of the 'Gladiator' Franchise

The "Gladiator" franchise, birthed from Ridley Scott's 2000 epic film, has left an indelible mark on popular culture and the film industry. As "Gladiator 2" prepares to continue this storied legacy, it's essential to reflect on the history of the franchise, its current status, and the potential avenues for its future. The journey of "Gladiator" from a singular cinematic triumph to a burgeoning franchise encapsulates a blend of historical grandeur, character-driven storytelling, and enduring cultural influence.

The Birth of a Legend

The original "Gladiator" film, released in 2000, was a critical and commercial triumph. It earned over $460 million worldwide and secured five Academy Awards, including Best Picture and Best Actor for Russell Crowe. The story of Maximus Decimus Meridius, a betrayed Roman general who seeks revenge against the corrupt emperor Commodus, resonated deeply with audiences. Ridley Scott's masterful direction, coupled with Hans Zimmer's evocative score and the film's groundbreaking visual effects, set new standards for historical epics.

Cultural Resonance: The film's influence extended beyond the box office and awards. Its portrayal of honor, loyalty, and vengeance struck a chord with viewers, embedding phrases like "Are you not entertained?" into the cultural lexicon. The film also reignited interest in ancient Roman history, influencing academic pursuits and popular media representations of the era.

Current Status: The Anticipation of 'Gladiator 2'

As the sequel to "Gladiator" approaches, the anticipation is a testament to the original film's enduring legacy. "Gladiator 2," directed once again by Ridley Scott, is set to continue the story, focusing on Lucius Verus, the nephew of Commodus, who was a child in the first film. Portrayed by Paul Mescal, Lucius's journey promises to explore themes of legacy, power, and redemption.

Plot and Character Development: "Gladiator 2" is expected to delve deeper into the political and social complexities of ancient Rome, offering a nuanced portrayal of its characters. The return of Connie Nielsen as Lucilla, alongside new characters played by Barry Keoghan and others, will add layers to the narrative, intertwining personal and political drama.

Technological Advances: The sequel benefits from two decades of advancements in film technology. The use of CGI and motion capture has evolved significantly, promising even more immersive recreations of ancient Rome. These technological strides will enhance the visual storytelling, making the epic battles and scenic vistas even more breathtaking.

The Franchise's Future: Potential Projects and Expansions

The success of "Gladiator 2" could pave the way for further expansions of the franchise, exploring different facets of the ancient world and its myriad stories. Here are some potential directions the franchise could take:

Television Series: With the rise of high-quality television series, the "Gladiator" franchise could expand into serialized storytelling. A TV series could explore various aspects of Roman society, from the political machinations of the Senate to the daily lives of gladiators and common citizens. Such a series could provide a more in-depth exploration of the era, offering rich character development and complex story arcs.

Spin-Off Films: The franchise could also explore spin-off films focusing on different characters or historical events within the same universe. For instance, a film centered on the rise and fall of the gladiatorial games, or a story about another legendary Roman figure, could expand the narrative scope while maintaining the thematic essence of "Gladiator."

Interactive Media: With advancements in virtual reality (VR) and augmented reality (AR), interactive experiences set in the world of "Gladiator" could become a reality. Imagine a VR experience where users can participate in gladiatorial combat or explore a meticulously recreated Roman city. These interactive experiences could offer an immersive way for fans to engage with the franchise.

Merchandising and Educational Partnerships: The "Gladiator" franchise could also expand through merchandising and educational initiatives. Collaborations with museums and educational institutions could result in exhibitions and learning programs that combine entertainment with historical education. Additionally, merchandise such as action figures, costumes, and detailed replicas could further entrench the franchise in popular culture.

The Legacy: Enduring Influence and Cultural Impact

The legacy of "Gladiator" extends beyond its direct contributions to film and media. It has influenced various aspects of pop culture, from fashion and fitness to language and academic interest.

Fashion and Fitness: The rugged, muscular physique of Russell Crowe's Maximus set new standards for male fitness in Hollywood. Gladiator-inspired fashion, such as strappy sandals and Roman-inspired accessories, also saw a resurgence following the film's release. This influence continues to be seen in contemporary fashion trends and fitness regimes.

Academic and Educational Impact: The film's historical setting spurred renewed interest in Roman history and culture. Universities and schools saw an uptick in enrollments in classical studies, and numerous documentaries and books were published exploring the historical accuracy of the film. "Gladiator" served as a gateway for many to explore the complexities and grandeur of ancient Rome.

Language and Expression: "Gladiator" enriched the cultural lexicon with memorable lines and phrases that are still quoted today. The film's dialogue has been referenced and parodied in various media, underscoring its lasting impact on language and expression.

Reflecting on the Franchise's Journey

The journey of the "Gladiator" franchise is a testament to the enduring power of storytelling. From its inception as a singular, groundbreaking film, it has grown into a cultural touchstone that continues to inspire and entertain. As we look forward to the release of "Gladiator 2" and beyond, it's clear that the franchise has the potential to evolve and expand, offering new stories and experiences that honor its legacy while forging new paths.

A Cultural Milestone: The original "Gladiator" film remains a cultural milestone, celebrated for its epic scope, powerful performances, and profound themes. Its influence on the film industry and popular culture is undeniable, and its legacy is carried forward by the anticipation and potential of its sequel.

The Future Awaits: As the franchise looks to the future, it stands at the crossroads of tradition and innovation. Whether through new films, television series, or interactive experiences, the world of "Gladiator" holds endless possibilities. The enduring appeal of its characters and themes ensures that it will continue to captivate and inspire audiences for years to come.

Conclusion

The legacy and future of the "Gladiator" franchise are intertwined with its profound impact on pop culture and the film industry. From the original film's groundbreaking achievements to the anticipation surrounding "Gladiator 2," the franchise exemplifies the power of epic storytelling. As it expands into new mediums and narratives, it promises to continue its cultural influence, inspiring future generations with tales of honor, courage, and the human spirit. The journey of "Gladiator" is far from over, and its echoes will undoubtedly resonate through the halls of cinematic history.

Conclusion
Final Thoughts and Predictions

As we draw the curtain on our exploration of "Gladiator 2," it's clear that this sequel holds immense promise, both as a continuation of a beloved story and as a potential game-changer in the film industry. The journey from the original "Gladiator" to this much-anticipated follow-up is a testament to the enduring power of epic storytelling, rich character development, and historical drama. Here, we reflect on the key points discussed and offer some final thoughts and predictions for the film's success and cultural impact.

Summary of Key Points

Revitalization of Historical Epics: "Gladiator 2" is set to reignite the historical epic genre, much like its predecessor did two decades ago. The original film not only captivated audiences with its grand storytelling and visual splendor but also set new benchmarks for the genre. With advancements in CGI and filmmaking techniques, the sequel is expected to push these boundaries even further, creating an immersive and visually stunning portrayal of ancient Rome.

Cultural and Fashion Influence: The original "Gladiator" left a lasting impact on fashion and pop culture, with its Roman-inspired designs influencing contemporary trends. "Gladiator 2" is poised to continue this legacy, potentially sparking new fashion trends and fitness regimes inspired by the characters' rugged, athletic physiques. The film's visual and thematic elements are likely to permeate various aspects of pop culture, from language to lifestyle.

Fan Engagement and Community: The anticipation for "Gladiator 2" has galvanized a vibrant fan community, evidenced by the plethora of fan art, community events, and online discussions. This engagement reflects a deep connection to the film's themes and characters, suggesting that the sequel will be embraced by both long-time fans and new audiences.

The continuation of Maximus's legacy through Lucius Verus provides a compelling narrative hook that resonates with viewers on multiple levels.

Technological and Cinematic Advancements: The use of advanced CGI and motion capture in "Gladiator 2" promises to deliver a cinematic experience that surpasses the original. These technological innovations will not only enhance the visual storytelling but also set new standards for future historical dramas. Ridley Scott's direction, combined with Hans Zimmer's evocative score, will create a powerful sensory experience that draws audiences into the world of ancient Rome.

Predicted Success and Cultural Impact:

Given the strong foundation laid by the original film and the current buzz surrounding the sequel, "Gladiator 2" is poised for significant success. Here are some predictions for its impact:

Box Office Success: "Gladiator 2" is likely to achieve substantial box office success, both domestically and internationally. The original film's legacy, coupled with the star power of the new cast and the anticipation built by effective marketing campaigns, will drive strong opening weekend numbers. The film's appeal to both fans of the original and new audiences will contribute to its sustained performance at the box office.

Critical Acclaim: The film is expected to receive critical acclaim for its storytelling, visual effects, and performances. Paul Mescal's portrayal of Lucius Verus and Barry Keoghan's performance as Sejanus are likely to be highlights, earning praise for their depth and complexity. Ridley Scott's direction and Hans Zimmer's score will also be key points of critical appreciation, reinforcing the film's artistic merits.

Awards and Recognition: "Gladiator 2" is poised to be a strong contender during awards season. The original film's success at the Oscars, combined with the sequel's high production values and compelling narrative, positions it well for nominations in major categories such as Best Picture, Best Director, and Best

Actor. The film's technical achievements in visual effects and sound design are also likely to be recognized.

Cultural Legacy: The sequel will likely cement the "Gladiator" franchise's place in cultural history. Its themes of honor, legacy, and the human struggle for justice will resonate with contemporary audiences, prompting discussions and reflections on these timeless concepts. The film's impact on fashion, fitness, and popular media will further extend its cultural footprint, ensuring that "Gladiator 2" leaves a lasting legacy.

Final Reflections

The journey from "Gladiator" to "Gladiator 2" reflects the evolution of storytelling, technology, and audience engagement over the past two decades. The original film's influence on the film industry and popular culture is undeniable, and the sequel is set to build on this legacy, offering a fresh yet familiar experience that honors its predecessor while exploring new narrative horizons.

As we await the film's release, the excitement and anticipation are palpable. "Gladiator 2" promises not only to entertain but also to inspire and provoke thought, much like the original did. The enduring appeal of its characters and themes ensures that it will continue to captivate audiences, leaving an indelible mark on the cultural landscape.

In conclusion, "Gladiator 2" is more than just a sequel; it is a testament to the power of epic storytelling and the enduring legacy of its predecessor. As the echoes of the Colosseum resonate once more, we are reminded of the timeless nature of its story and the universal appeal of its themes. The film stands poised to achieve great success, both critically and commercially, and its impact will be felt for years to come. Whether through its cinematic achievements, cultural influence, or the passion of its fan community, "Gladiator 2" is set to solidify its place in the pantheon of great films, echoing in eternity as a modern epic.

What to Look Forward To

As the release of "Gladiator 2" draws near, anticipation is mounting for what promises to be one of the most thrilling cinematic experiences of the year. Ridley Scott returns to the director's chair, ready to transport audiences once again to the grandeur and brutality of ancient Rome. Fans of the original film, as well as newcomers, have much to look forward to in this epic sequel. Here's a detailed look at the key elements and exciting aspects that make "Gladiator 2" a film to be genuinely enthusiastic about.

A Return to Rome: Cinematic Brilliance

One of the most compelling reasons to be excited about "Gladiator 2" is the promise of a visually stunning return to ancient Rome. Ridley Scott's mastery in creating immersive, historically rich worlds ensures that viewers will once again be treated to the awe-inspiring sights of the Roman Empire. The film's use of cutting-edge CGI, combined with meticulously designed practical sets, will bring the Colosseum, Roman streets, and palatial estates to life with unprecedented detail.

Expect sweeping vistas of the Roman countryside, grand architectural feats, and the visceral intensity of the gladiatorial arena. The film's cinematography, likely to be lush and expansive, will capture both the epic scale and the intimate moments of the story, providing a feast for the eyes.

Compelling Characters: New and Familiar Faces

The characters in "Gladiator 2" are set to drive the narrative forward with depth and complexity. Paul Mescal stars as Lucius Verus, the grown-up nephew of Commodus and the central figure in this new chapter. Mescal's portrayal promises to be a nuanced exploration of a young man grappling with the legacy of Maximus Decimus Meridius and his own path to honor and leadership. Early buzz suggests Mescal's performance will be both commanding and emotionally resonant, anchoring the film's dramatic arcs.

Fans can also look forward to the return of Connie Nielsen as Lucilla, bringing continuity and depth to the story. Barry Keoghan's Sejanus, the film's antagonist, is expected to add layers of intrigue and tension. Keoghan is known for his intense and captivating performances, and his role as Sejanus is likely to be a standout, adding a sinister edge to the political and personal conflicts at play.

Epic Storytelling: Themes of Legacy and Redemption

"Gladiator 2" delves into themes of legacy, power, and redemption, offering a rich narrative tapestry that will resonate with audiences. The story picks up two decades after the original, focusing on Lucius's journey as he navigates the complex political landscape of Rome and his personal quest for honor. The film explores the weight of Maximus's legacy, the struggles for power, and the pursuit of justice in a corrupt world.

This thematic depth, combined with the high stakes of the narrative, promises a gripping and emotionally engaging story. The film's exploration of personal and political drama, set against the backdrop of historical events, will provide a compelling and thought-provoking viewing experience.

Spectacular Action Sequences

The original "Gladiator" set a high bar for action sequences, and "Gladiator 2" is poised to exceed it. The film promises intense, well-choreographed combat scenes that will capture the brutal reality of gladiatorial battles. Fans can expect edge-of-the-seat moments as Lucius and other characters face life-and-death struggles in the arena, with choreography that combines historical authenticity and cinematic flair.

The action sequences will not only serve as thrilling spectacles but also as pivotal narrative moments that reveal character and drive the story forward. The combination of physicality, strategy, and raw emotion in these scenes will ensure that they are memorable highlights of the film.

A Stirring Score by Hans Zimmer

Hans Zimmer's return as the composer for "Gladiator 2" is another major highlight. Zimmer's original score for "Gladiator" remains iconic, and his music for the sequel is expected to be equally powerful and evocative. The soundtrack will blend familiar motifs with new compositions, enhancing the film's emotional depth and epic scope.

Zimmer's ability to craft music that resonates deeply with audiences will elevate the film's dramatic moments and action sequences. Fans of the original score can look forward to new musical themes that capture the spirit of "Gladiator" while adding fresh, stirring elements to the auditory experience.

Innovative Visual Effects and Technology

"Gladiator 2" will leverage the latest advancements in visual effects and technology to create a more immersive and realistic portrayal of ancient Rome. The use of advanced CGI and motion capture will bring the grandeur of Roman architecture, the chaos of battle, and the intricacies of character interactions to life with stunning clarity and realism.

These technological innovations will not only enhance the visual spectacle but also allow for more dynamic and fluid storytelling. The film's ability to blend practical effects with digital artistry will set new standards for historical epics, making it a visual and technical marvel.

Community and Cultural Impact

The release of "Gladiator 2" is set to be a major cultural event, bringing together fans of the original film and attracting new audiences. The excitement and buzz generated by the film will foster a vibrant community of fans, eager to discuss and celebrate its themes, characters, and visual achievements.

Moreover, the film's exploration of historical and ethical themes will prompt discussions and reflections that extend beyond the cinema. The cultural impact of "Gladiator 2" will be felt in academic circles, popular media, and fan communities, ensuring that its legacy continues to grow and inspire.

Final Thoughts

As "Gladiator 2" approaches its release, there is much to be enthusiastic about. The film promises to deliver a visually stunning and emotionally compelling continuation of a beloved story, driven by strong performances, epic storytelling, and innovative filmmaking. Fans can look forward to a rich narrative that explores themes of legacy and redemption, spectacular action sequences, a stirring score by Hans Zimmer, and the latest advancements in visual effects.

"Gladiator 2" stands poised to not only honor the legacy of the original film but also to carve out its own place in cinematic history. It promises to be a cultural and artistic milestone, offering a powerful and immersive experience that will captivate audiences around the world. Whether you are a long-time fan of the original or a newcomer to the saga, "Gladiator 2" is a film that deserves a place on your must-watch list.

Printed in Great Britain
by Amazon